MOTHER NATURE'S

GREATEST HITS

THE TOP 40 WONDERS OF THE ANIMAL WORLD

by
Bartleby Nash

illustrated by
Ptolemy Tompkins

LIVING PLANET
PRESS

Los Angeles

Published in the United States by Living Planet Press,
558 Rose Avenue, Venice, California 90291

Distributed by Publishers Group West, Emeryville, California

The author is grateful for permission to include the following previously copyrighted
material:

Quotations on pages 13-14 and 68: copyright © 1967 by Jacques Graven from
the book *Non-Human Thought,* originally published and translated in
the English language by Stein & Day, Inc., reprinted with permission of
Scarborough House/Publishers.

Quotations on pages 44 and 91-92: from *Wild Heritage* by Sally Carrighar,
copyright © 1965 by Sally Carrighar, reprinted by permission of Houghton
Mifflin Co.

Quotations on page 73: reprinted with permission of Guinness Publishing,
from *Animal Facts and Feats* by Gerald L. Wood, copyright © Gerald Wood
and Guinness Superlatives Ltd 1982.

Quotations on pages 76 and 86: reprinted with permission of Charles Scribner's
Sons, an imprint of Macmillan Publishing Co., from *Just Like an Animal* by
Maurice Burton, copyright © 1978 Maurice Burton.

Interior design and page layout: Karen Bowers
Printing and binding: The Banta Company

ISBN 0-9626072-7-4

Discounts for bulk orders are available from the publisher. Call (213) 396-0188.

Printed on recycled paper

Manufactured in the United States of America
Library of Congress catalog card number 90-064449

10   9   8   7   6   5   4   3   2   1

MOTHER NATURE'S TOP 40

FOREWORD

The animal kingdom provides an endless source of amusement and fascination for the casual observer – a flotilla of fuzzy goslings following its parents through a pond, a house cat stalking its prey as gracefully as a lioness, the elegant design of a spider's web or a zebra's markings.

But an even more profound sensation rewards those who investigate further – the mystery and wonder of being brought face to face with the unknown and the unknowable: the mysteries of migration, the miracles of evolution and adaptation, the intractable force of instinct. Where else but in the animal world can we find so many of life's unanswerable questions posed so abundantly?

In *Mother Nature's Greatest Hits,* you'll learn the secrets of the shark's digestive tract, the meaning of the bowerbird's legendary courtship dance, the truth behind elephant intelligence and the talents of the giant squid. You'll even discover the natural phenomena responsible for animals raining down from the heavens.

But the answers this book provides are really less significant than the questions it raises. The more we study the astounding range and diversity of animal life and behavior on this planet, the more wondrous and unfathomable Mother Nature's creation appears. Yet every day, whole species disappear forever from the face of the earth. And when they vanish into extinction, their unique contribution to the grand experiment of life on this planet vanishes with them.

Whether these *Top 40 Wonders of the Animal World* make you laugh, shudder or shake your head in disbelief, I hope they give you pause to consider how closely our human fate is intertwined with the fate of the animals who share our planet. While nature trivia is a great source of amusement, the reawakening of appreciation for our kinship with the natural world is certainly one of the least trivial tasks confronting us.

I invite you to laugh, delight and marvel at the natural wonders of our world – and then to join us in working to preserve them in all their glory.

— Kathryn S. Fuller
President, World Wildlife Fund

A BOLT FROM THE BLUE

Glacier Fleas, Stoic Snails and the Beginnings of Life

Life here on earth has apparently been going on for an incredibly long time – about three-and-a-half billion years by general scientific consensus. But for the first three billion of those years, such life as there was did not take very imposing forms. A time traveler with mask and snorkel would find almost no visible evidence of life beneath the waters of the world until about 700 million years ago, at which point the scenery would have been enlivened by some worms and jellyfish. Before that, the only non-microscopic form of life on hand – the single large-scale piece of evidence that organic processes were afoot – was something called a stromatolite. Stromatolites are round, bottom-growing collections of primitive algae that in fossilized form look more or less like cabbages. For millions upon millions of years, these little "forests" of algae growing on the sunlit floors of shallow seas were the biggest, flashiest examples of living matter the earth had to offer.

No one knows what the earth's first example of microscopic life looked like or where and how in the ancient seas it got started. Many still hold to the familiar theory that a lightning bolt striking the surface of the ocean somehow or other zapped a bunch of organic molecules in such a way that they fell into a formation that permitted them to take in energy from the outside world, grow and reproduce. Others argue that even the simplest known form of life is so intensely complex that the probability of an electrical current generating it, even once, from a random collection of matter is about as likely as a similar bolt of lightning today creating a three-story building by striking a pile of bricks.

Some years ago a group of scientists, wrestling with the question of whether we and all our fellow creatures really did originate from a well-aimed lightning bolt, conducted a series of experiments to see if they could repeat such an event under laboratory conditions. They assembled a number of organic chemicals that they believed to have been present in the air and sea at the time of life's inception and blasted them with electricity. Some of the resulting super-charged ooze actually did turn out to resemble that very primitive form of plant life called algae, but as the stuff proved incapable of replicating itself, it ultimately failed to qualify as living – for all life, by definition, reproduces.

In the beginning

The greatest wonder of the natural world may be the existence of life itself. So incredible was the achievement of "simple" organic life on earth that some reputable scientists insist it must have come from elsewhere – "elsewhere" meaning outer space. But this theory doesn't come much closer to solving the puzzle. Instead, it only pushes it momentarily out of the way. For if outer space is the ultimate place of life's origin, the question still lingers: How did it get started out there?

From whatever or wherever it did come, life is now so pervasively established on our planet that there is almost nowhere it can't be found in one form or another. Some primitive life forms get all the nutrition they need from eating single, obscure elements such as platinum. More advanced creatures, such as the famous drugstore beetle, can live in, breathe and consume highly toxic substances that would kill other animals in seconds. Bacteria, and even some fish, live in waters that approach boiling, while the glacier flea of the deep Arctic is capable of subsisting on, well...glaciers.

In addition to surviving in all but the harshest of habitats, some of the earth's life forms are capable of doing without the most basic of needs – food and moisture, for example – for extremely long periods of time. Some birds and many mammals are capable of slowing their metabolic processes to far below their normal rates during periods of hibernation or semi-hibernation. Certain fish and insects can survive being frozen solid or dried up like apricots. One stoic snail was mistaken for dead and kept on exhibit at the American Museum of Natural History for three years before rousing itself and breaking free from the placard to which it had been attached.

INSTINCTIVE ABSURDITIES

Bouncing Sheep and Instincts Gone Awry

What we call "instinct" remains another great mystery to science. Defined simply, instinct means behavior that hasn't been learned but which Mother Nature has "built into" her offspring. Some animals, especially the insects, operate almost entirely by means of

4

instinctive programming, while the higher animals – especially we humans – manage to escape being totally dominated by it, or so we'd like to think.

As a general rule, the less brain an animal carries, the more it relies on instinctive be- haviors to cope with the challenges of day-to-day living. It's extremely difficult, for example, to train an ant to act in un- antlike ways. Yet it's comparatively easy to teach an intelligent animal like a dog or a chimpanzee to forego old behaviors and adopt new ones.

Famous followers

As essential as instinct may be for animal and human survival, however, there are times when an automatic reaction can be more hindrance than help. Even reasonably intelligent animals which should know better can find themselves in situations where deeply ingrained habits of response force them to act in ridiculous ways. Animal writer Frank W. Lane gives several amusing examples of instinct gone awry.

One typical example of instinctive behavior persisting beyond the point of necessity, as Lane sees it, is sometimes witnessed among domestic sheep. In times past, when the sheep's wild ancestors relied upon their mountain-climbing ability to escape from predators, they appear to have developed what could be called a "follow-the-leader instinct." This behavior served them well when negotiating narrow, treacherous passes. Because only the head sheep could get a clear view of the difficult terrain ahead, those who followed learned to imitate the leader's movements exactly, regardless of whether they could see the action's purpose. Just like their

5

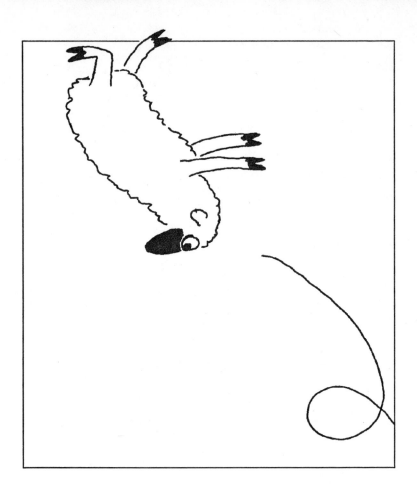

ancestors, domestic sheep will sometimes fall into the habit of doing whatever the sheep in front of them does, whether it makes sense or not.

This habit was first discovered by the British naturalist E. Kay Robinson when, as a child, he watched a flock of sheep being herded through a narrow gate. Stretching his leg across the opening, Robinson created a barrier that the sheep could only negotiate by making a quick jump. The first animal halted in bewilderment for a moment, then made the necessary jump. The sheep behind followed the leader's example when they came to the spot and continued to do so even after Robinson removed his leg. After several minutes, the bouncing step caught on until the whole flock was pointlessly hopping up and down.

Double trouble

Of the many examples of misplaced instinct that Lane presents, the most bizarre is probably that of the two-headed snake. A number of these schizophrenic reptiles have been kept in captivity, where they have been observed to indulge their aggressive instincts with disastrous results. An unsupervised two-headed snake will sooner or later start quarreling with itself. Head number one will try to bite and swallow head number two and vice versa, in what is obviously a no-win situation.

MOTHER NATURE'S
GREATEST HITS

3

KEEN SENSORS

The Dog's Nose, the Bat's Ear,
the Housefly's Compound Eye

Though we far outdistance them when it comes to "higher order" capacities – such as dealing with meaning, destiny, good, evil and other such weighty abstractions – most animals are much more sensitive to the physical world than we are. The universe in which we all live is a radically different place for most animals than it is for us, and the task of envisioning how the world appears to them is one of the biggest challenges for the human imagination.

Anyone who has spent some time with dogs knows that they have very different ideas about which aspects of the outside world are worthy of investigation. The sight of a dog straining on its leash to investigate every shrub and lamppost on a single city block is a vivid reminder of how much of the physical world we miss. Because a dog's sense of smell is many times more powerful than ours, that seemingly ordinary stretch of concrete appears to him as a lush and tantalizingly complicated web of exciting and suggestive information.

First-class ears and compound eyes

Equally alien universes open up for those creatures that rely most heavily on sound to get around. Much has been learned recently about the "sound picture" that bats, whales, dolphins and other animals experience by means of echolocation (which, very roughly, is the emission of sounds that bounce off distant objects to reveal their size, their shape and even their texture). The mechanics of this process are now very well understood, and humans have even figured out how to construct machines that operate on the same principle. Yet even with a good abstract understanding of how this method of perception works, it's hard to comprehend how some animals "see" their world in just as great detail through their ears as we do through our eyes. A dolphin, for example, can tell the difference between a penny and a dime lying on the floor of its darkened tank with no

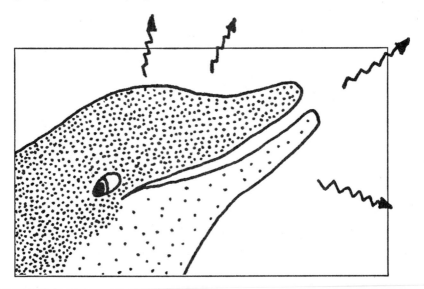

great effort, and a bat can maneuver through a maze of hanging nets in total darkness with equal ease.

Even the visual dimension in which we humans feel most at home is a far richer domain for many creatures than it is for us. If hawks knew how to read, they could scan a page of *War and Peace* from a rooftop perch. Their eyes have been designed to pick up the precise outlines of small prey animals on the ground from far above.

Our eyes are also unable to process light waves that many insects have no trouble registering. Infrared and ultraviolet light exist outside the limits of the visible spectrum for humans, unless aided by complex optical devices. Insects, however, live in a world dominated by these frequencies. Many species perceive their world of different hues by means of multiple, unblinking eyes that process visual information in a manner quite unlike our own. An insect such as a housefly receives, at every moment, not a single, unified picture of the world around it but hundreds of separate ones from each of its multifaceted compound eyes. How does the miniscule housefly brain make sense of, and successfully act upon, this constant rush of multiple images? To answer that, one would have to be a housefly.

MOTHER NATURE'S
GREATEST HITS

4

SMART TALKERS

Polly Wants a Speaking Part

Birds are notoriously talkative animals. The "vocabularies" of some species have as many as several hundred distinct sounds and phrases, some of them surprisingly sophisticated. The crows of the world share the same general repertoire of sounds, but some populations are more eloquent than others – both in terms of size of vocabulary and the "dialect" in which it is expressed.

Science tends to divide the various types of bird-speak into two general categories. When a bird makes a noise, the theory goes, it's either producing a "call" or a "song." Most birdcalls are made with specific ends in mind – locating other birds or warning of an approaching enemy – while bird song is a more mysterious phenomenon. Though most bird songs can also be more or less explained as arising from such needs as the defense of territory and the wooing of members of the opposite sex, some species seem to sing purely for the fun of it. The old question of why birds sing may never be entirely answered by science – if it needs to be answered at all.

Birdbrained conversation

With birds, as with humans, a pretty voice doesn't always indicate intelligence. The subtlety and nuance of crow speech often goes unnoticed because it's not as immediately appealing as the far less sophisticated call of a whippoorwill or mourning dove. But with some species – especially the parrots and the mynahs – the ability to memorize and replicate complex sounds and phrasings is so developed that humans have forgiven them for the brassy, obnoxious tone in which they are so often delivered.

In *Non-Human Thought*, Jacques Graven collected some of the most outstanding examples of parrot and mynah mimicry – examples that suggest there might be a lot more going on in the brains of birds than one might assume. Jaco, an African grey parrot who lived in the city of Salzberg about a hundred years ago, not only knew many human words and phrases but also when and where to apply them. Jaco's owner once presented him with a young partridge which, after becoming comfortable in its new surroundings, began to sing. At this, Jaco is reliably said to have commented "Bravo, little one, bravo!"

Another African grey, named Coco, is said by Graven to have spoken competently in Dutch, French and German. Apparently not content with the bird's impressive mastery of

human speech, one of Coco's human acquaintances once tried to teach him some rudimentary acrobatics. After being commanded to leap up on a perch a few times, Coco got the idea of what was being asked of him but instead of complying, addressed the man in question by name and commanded *him* to get up on the perch. Graven does not mention in which of Coco's several languages this exchange took place.

As impressive as Graven's parrot tales are, they pale in comparison to his report on the achievements of a trio of mynah birds who, for a time, lived side by side in a pet shop.

"These birds," writes Graven, "were particularly loud-mouthed. While one of them imitated the sound of dishes being smashed, the second would yell, 'Cut it out, now, shut your trap!' and the third would chime in, 'You too, banana-head!' The time came when this extraordinary trio had to be split up. The mynah which had been sold was carried out through the pet shop door, without any hope of coming back. To the amazement of all concerned, before disappearing, he turned back and, with a last look at the pet shop saleswoman and his playmates, called out: 'Good-bye, mother, good bye, old pals!'"

Could such an astonishing trio really have existed, and did they really come up with all these impressive quips? Well...maybe. It all depends on how much credit one is willing to extend to the bird brain.

The singing mouse phenomenon

Human beings have always had a special fondness for animals that indulge in weird, quirky behaviors that science can't explain. Many people who claim to dislike mice, for example, might change their minds if they encountered one that knew how to sing. A number of mouse species occasionally produce individuals with voices capable of complex and pleasant sounding melodies. The ability doesn't seem to be inherited nor to be of much practical use, but that doesn't stop such gifted individuals from exercising their talents. A white-footed mouse kept as a pet during the nineteenth century is reported to have enjoyed singing so much that it "carrolled almost incessantly." This particular mouse is said to have possessed a repertoire of different songs, including a tune its owner called the "wheel-song" because it was sung exclusively while the mouse was running on its exercise wheel.

Opinions differ on exactly what a singing mouse sounds like. Its voice has been described as a "warble," a "whistle," a "kind of to-wit-to-wee-woo-woo-wee-woo," and a "rollicking chuckling very like a boy, whistling as he runs, drawing a stick along the pickets of a fence."

What most witnesses of the singing mouse phenomenon do agree upon is the singular beauty of the tune produced. The owner of the white-footed specimen mentioned above found his pet's voice so pleasant that he would lie down after a hard day and listen appreciatively to his "wee songster, whose cage I had set by my bedside. To be sure, it was a low, very low, sweet voice. But there was, with a singular weirdness, something so sweetly merry, that I would listen on, and on, until I would fall asleep in the lullaby of my wingless and quadropedal bob-o'-link."

BIG MAMAS

A Whale of a Growth Spurt

Everything that lives must grow to some extent, but there is an enormous variation in how – and how fast – the process is accomplished. Plants tend to grow a lot faster than animals because they mainly rely on stretching cells that already exist instead of the much slower process of creating new ones. Seaweed grows extremely fast, and the rubbery giant kelps of Pacific waters can ultimately reach 900 feet in length. Bamboo doesn't get as large as kelp, but it grows faster: as much as forty-seven inches in only twenty-four hours.

Among animals, the record for speedy growth probably

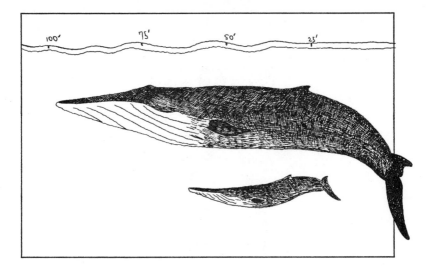

belongs to the blue whale, which also happens to be the largest animal that has ever existed on earth. Baby blue whales are already around twenty-five feet at birth. In the process of reaching their adult length of 100 feet or more, they pass through periods in which they can grow faster than an inch-and-a-half in length per day. This comparatively massive daily increase in length is complemented by an equally enormous increase in weight: as much as 200 pounds in twenty-four hours.

PEOPLE-EATERS

Claws and Jaws of Ill Repute

The biggest land-dwelling carnivore in the world is either the polar bear or the brown bear, depending on whom you ask. The distinction isn't that important because the two creatures are so closely related that the polar bear can be thought of as a special version of the brown bear adapted for a marine environment. Both animals are direct descendants of the cave bear, a massively built vegetarian which lived in the days when our ancestors prowled the world with stone-tipped spears.

Polar bears are very recent inventions – perhaps only about 50,000 years old – and are still in the process of adapting themselves to the Arctic wasteland of drifting ice in which they have chosen to spend their lives. Unlike other bears, the polar bear is a strict meat eater. Seals make up the bulk of its diet.

Since the slippery seal is too swift and agile to be caught underwater, the bear must use its wits to take its prey by surprise on land. Polar bears are not only good at sneaking up on seals; they can sneak up on human beings in the same way. Many an early Arctic explorer met their end at the paws of polar bears quite literally without knowing what hit them.

The combination of the polar bear's massive size and its ability to creep delicately right up to the heels of oblivious humans have combined to include it among the most feared of all land animals. Even the Eskimos, who spend their lives among bears, never feel entirely at ease when they are out hunting on

the pack ice, for polar bears have been known to stalk humans for days at a time – sometimes with the intent of making a meal of them and sometimes apparently just for the sport of putting humans in compromising and uncomfortable positions.

Don't go near the water

The polar bear isn't the only animal which consistently refuses to run in terror from humans, and it isn't the only one that eats them on occasion, either. Lions, tigers and a handful of other land animals are also worthy of a respectful distance. The likeliest place to get eaten by a fellow creature, however, is probably in the water.

The impressively proportioned great white shark, which grows to at least twenty feet and may reach lengths as great as thirty, is no doubt the most publicized people-eater in the animal kingdom. These animals don't eat humans with great regularity, but when the habit strikes them, they carry it out with such gusto that the event lingers long in human memory. Even a "small" great white shark – such as the eight-footer that killed several people off the coast of New Jersey in 1916 – is capable of inflicting such massive damage that great white attacks are often fatal. To add to its fearsome reputation, this creature has a habit of sticking its enormous head out of the water and gnashing its jaws at observers in boats. Some cases have even been reported of great white sharks attacking and sinking small crafts.

Killer whales lack the great white's undiscerning ferocity and rarely act aggressively towards humans, but that does not mean they necessarily fear our kind. In times past, these intelligent aquatic mammals sometimes "collaborated" with whalers by herding their larger cousins into the paths of harpoon boats. One such partnership between a pod of killers and a small Pacific whaling fleet went on for more than a decade, with what could only be called a friendship springing up between the human and cetacean predators.

Of the very small number of animals that regularly harass and devour humans, the most audacious is the salt-water, or estuarine, crocodile. These imposing remnants from the age of the dinosaurs average about fifteen feet in length at maturity. In the days before hunting by indignant humans thinned their

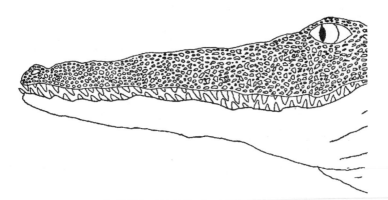

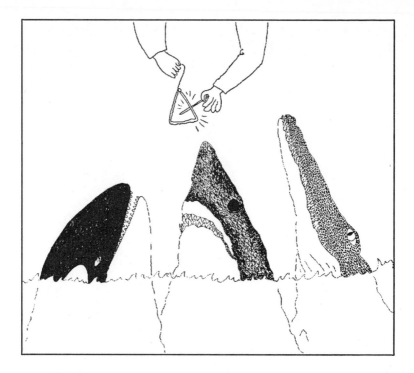

numbers, some specimens might have grown to twice that size. The salt-water crocodile does not have to be pressed to eat people; the habit comes naturally. Even with its reduced numbers, this creature manages to account for a fair number of deaths. The writer Gerald L. Wood states that as many as 2,000 people still perish in the jaws of the estuarine crocodile each year.

In addition to humans, this fearsome reptile has been known to prey on a number of other animals who aren't used to being made into meals. Wood sites one case in which a healthy, adult rhinoceros was seen being dragged into the depths.

FUN LOVERS

Dolphins, Sea Otters and Other
Champions of Pointless Play

Play is serious business for kids, takes up half a page in the dictionary and is intuitively understood by old and young alike. But what is this thing called play, really?

For humans, the line between playful and non-playful behavior is extremely fuzzy. It's easy to see that two boys tossing a football back and forth are playing. But a few years down the line, when those same young men join a high-school football

23

team and compete in games before bleachers full of people, the implications of throwing and catching may change dramatically. The activity of propelling the ball toward one another that was originally performed for its own sake is now colored by a host of serious, goal-oriented objectives such as making touchdowns, impressing girls and winning football scholarships. A pursuit that was once simple and carefree becomes something more akin to work.

The same is true of animal behavior. Lion cubs pouncing on the twitching tail of a lounging adult, or adolescent wolves playing tag with one another are not only enjoying themselves but practicing techniques that they will later use to attack and kill other animals for food. Some experts have gone so far as to suggest that there is really no such thing as "pure" play in the animal world – that every action, no matter how frivolous it may seem, can always be understood as a way to enhance the animal's chances for survival.

For those who dislike the idea that all of nature is one big goal-oriented, no-nonsense machine, there are a number of animals that regularly indulge in forms of play that appear to be so patently worthless in terms of survival value that they are

difficult to justify in practical terms. To cite three examples from Sally Carrighar's book, *Wild Heritage:* Why do badgers perform somersaults and play leap-frog with each other, except for fun? Could a hummingbird which repeatedly rides downstream on a cascade of water pouring from a garden hose be practicing to ride a waterfall? And what about wild buffalos of times past who were recorded leaping into rivers from low bluffs – were they practicing evasive techniques or just enjoying the splash? Even the ever-hungry, over-anxious shrew will take time out to invent games if provided with enough readily available food that it can take its mind off hunting.

Whales and dolphins are well-known for their playful antics. Dolphins often ride on the bow waves created by boats. In the times before boats existed, they used the turbulence created by whales for the same purpose. In the boredom of

captivity, dolphins and certain kinds of whales will take to "posing" in odd positions and copying the actions of other animals, including humans that enter their tank. After watching the mating activities of a group of fur seals that shared its tank, for example, one group of dolphins had fun imitating the seals' gyrations with one another.

The most persistently playful of all animals is probably the California sea otter. Like most other animals, sea otters must meet the challenges of securing food, avoiding enemies and raising their young. Yet these creatures manage to spend much of their waking time involved in gratuitous play of one kind or another – from games of tag to surfing sessions to benign harassment of other more slow-witted sea creatures. The definition of play may be difficult for humans to pin down, but the sea otter and many other creatures are having too much fun playing to care.

GREAT PRETENDERS

Bat Bluffers, Sausage Trees and the Mussel's Masquerade

One of the most puzzling and provocative of Mother Nature's traits is the way her various creations manage to avoid being eaten by one another through the use of creative deception. How is it, for example, that certain species of non-poisonous snakes have come to resemble their poisonous cousins so closely that they are given a wide berth by carnivorous birds and mammals that prey on poisonous varieties? How did certain species of caterpillars manage to alter the shape and color of their bodies so they look exactly like bird droppings and so are passed over by insect-eating predators?

The usual explanation for such phenomena is that of natural selection – that over the course of millions of years of haphazard experimentation, earth's creatures slowly but inevitably arrived at the designs that were most conducive to their own longevity. According to this theory, certain moths which, by a genetic fluke, just happened to resemble a heap of bird guano, stood a better chance of surviving than their more conventional-looking brothers and sisters, and hence were more likely to live long enough to reproduce.

For about a hundred years – ever since the theory of evolution was put forth by Charles Darwin in his *Origin of Species* – this simple but elegant idea has been used to explain all of the endlessly intricate forms and behaviors that living things have developed to increase their chances of survival. Most scientists still hold to it religiously, but a few have dared to suggest that while natural selection unquestionably plays a large part in shaping all organic life, it may not tell the whole story.

The cleverest pretenders

Many animal adaptations are so intricately contrived that it would seem impossible – no matter how many millions of years were involved – that they could have developed purely by random experimentation. Nowhere is this better illustrated than with the more unusual techniques that plants, bugs and animals use to deceive one another.

One species of caterpillar, for example, discourages other animals from eating it by "pretending" that it has already been eaten by another animal and vomited back up. Certain moths are able to alter the frequency of their wing beats so they won't register on the sonar picture that bats use to track them. The sausage tree, which grows in Africa and relies not on birds or bugs but bats for pollination, attracts these creatures by generating an odor of carrion or musk, which the bats find irresistible.

In the shallows of certain lakes, there is a species of

freshwater mussel that employs a unique scheme for the incubation and transportation of its young. The female mussel grows a full-scale, anatomically accurate model of a certain kind of fish along the top of its shell which will attract fish of that species. While investigating the decoy, a fish takes some of the mussel's larvae into its mouth. The larvae end up in the fish's gills and remain there until the fish expels its stowaways to be deposited in another part of the lake.

How did molluscs come to masquerade as fish, caterpillars begin to resemble vomit, and trees start to smell like musk? Some have guessed at the basis for these strange adaptations, but at present, these explanations, along with many others, remain locked away in Mother Nature's library of mysteries.

AMAZING ADAPTERS

Octopus Eyes, Woodpecker Tongues and Other Evolutionary Riddles

One of the animals most frequently brought up in discussions of the limitations of the theory of natural selection is the woodpecker. A woodpecker spends its life pecking holes in the bark of trees to dislodge the insects that live inside them. Having pecked its hole, the bird gropes around inside it with an extremely long tongue covered with a sticky substance that acts as flypaper to the hapless insects inside the tree. The woodpecker's tongue is so long in relation to its head that when not in use, it must be "stored" in a most unusual fashion. The

tongue itself originates not in the throat but in the base of the woodpecker's bill, twining through the bones of the skull in an intricate and extremely bizarre fashion.

According to some scientists, this unique design system could not have gradually evolved from a more conventionally designed tongue, but would have had to assume its peculiar design all in one step. It's easy enough to understand, for example, how the whale's terrestrial ancestors slowly changed their bodies into a more streamlined form after spending millions of years sloshing around in the water. But the leap that the woodpecker's tongue underwent seems a bit too far-flung for natural selection. It appears, instead, that the necessary modifications were made in one fell swoop, without the appearance of any in-between models.

Like man, like squid

Throwing another wrench into the theory of natural selection, one group of invertebrates that would seem to share very few qualities with humans enjoys a surprising similarity to us in at least one respect. As with so many other animal groups, squids and octopi once enjoyed an evolutionary heyday during which there were a great many more of their own kind swimming around than there are at present. In those times, most cephalopods (or "head-foots") carried delicately tapered shells that either spiraled around like those of snails or stretched straight back like giant ice-cream cones. Fossilized specimens of these shells have been found to measure as long as fifteen feet. It would have been an impressive sight, indeed, to witness one of these multi-armed, bug-eyed supersnails rocketing through the waters.

Today, all of the remaining cephalopods – with the exception of the six species of the chambered nautilus which still jet and hover around the waters of the South Pacific – have given up their protective shells. It is probably this change which prompted these most alien of creatures to develop eyes that, in design and function, are closer to our own than those of any other animal. Both the squid and the octopus can focus sharply on small objects, an ability lacking in many other animals, including some of our fellow mammals.

While not identical, the structures of the human and the cephalopod eye are similar enough to raise puzzling questions about the forces which drive and shape the process of evolution. The human eye is one of nature's most sophisticated and beautifully designed pieces of equipment that is thought by some to have taken millions of years of "blind" trial and error to perfect. Yet looking at the squid and the octopus, we see that this fabulous device was already being used by creatures very different from us millions of years before our remotest ancestors set foot on land. In other words, it seems that the basic design of the human eye was "invented" by Mother Nature not once, but twice.

Eyes aren't the only design feature that sets octopi and squid apart from their fellow sea-creatures. The cephalopod brain – especially that of the octopus – is extraordinarily well-developed, so much so that the smarter octopus species rival mammals such as cats in terms of intelligence. Next to the cetaceans, the octopus is the brightest creature in the sea, which is quite an achievement for an animal that doesn't even have a backbone.

SEX AND DEATH

Mating Microbes and Other Wonders of Reproduction

In the earliest days of life on earth, before the art of trading genetic material had been perfected, every new single-celled organism that came into being had exactly the same genetic make-up as the parent organism from which it had split off, and thus in essence was not really a new organism at all. With the introduction of sexual reproduction, quick to become the dominant form of reproduction on earth, came the possibility of an offspring that was not simply a carbon copy of its parent but an altogether new creature – an individual with its own entirely unique genetic make-up.

The essence of sex in all its astounding (to say the least) variety of forms is the transmission of genetic material from one organism to another. This activity seems to have been practiced by unicellular organisms long before life had begun to divide itself into such basic components as plant and animal. While a very few organisms reproduce without the transfer of genetic material that sex implies (either by simply splitting in half or by sprouting little versions of themselves out of their sides in a process called "budding"), the vast majority of animals practice genuine sexual reproduction at least on occasion. From the relatively straightforward gene-swapping that takes place when two bacteria cells rub up against each other to the phantasmagoric dramas practiced by humans and their fellow higher animals, sex not only makes it possible for life to grow and evolve but in one way or another lies behind a great many of the countless daily intrigues that have been unfolding since the beginning of life on earth.

One of a kind

It is only with individuality that true and irrevocable death enters the picture. Single-celled, asexually reproducing creatures are, in the words of Joseph Wood Krutch, "potentially immortal," because no matter how many of them are destroyed in the course of each hazardous day of life on earth, there are still countless other identical versions of that creature floating around elsewhere. Each one of these is itself constantly splitting and creating more versions of itself, to the point where there are so many clones in existence that it would take a truly monumental catastrophe to wipe them all out.

The case is entirely different for a creature produced by sexual reproduction. A possum killed while crossing a highway or a mosquito crushed in the act of drawing blood from somebody's arm might be replaced in the scheme of things by other possums and mosquitos. But those two individual, particular creatures – with their very personal, unique and unrepeatable genetic characteristics – are gone forever.

PLUMED SUITORS

Bowerbirds, Ostriches and Other Bird Romancers

Attracting members of the opposite sex is a sizable challenge for many groups of animals besides humans. While insects have given the act of sex itself a boggling variety of unlikely twists and turns, birds definitely have the edge on courtship. Mating displays – generally performed by the male for the benefit of a female audience – are popular throughout the bird world.

Peacocks may be best known for their extravagant fans of blue-green tail feathers proudly displayed for the sole purpose of impressing prospective peahens. The loons of America's northern lakes go to even greater lengths, performing extraordinary water dances to attract their loon-mates. In addition to dancing, singing and elaborate feather unfurlings, bird courtship may involve a presentation of gifts. Terns proffer small fish to their prospective mates, while down in the frigid Antarctic, courting penguins present carefully chosen pebbles as trousseau gifts.

Another outstanding aspect of bird courtship is the passion and fury that the males of many species generate in the days leading up to the conjugal event. A male ostrich, which can stand as tall as eight feet and weigh up to 300 pounds, can get so worked up that he may pose a serious threat to any humans in

the area. In one report, an impassioned male mistook a passing train for a rival and charged furiously at it. Not surprisingly, the train won.

The greatest architect of love

Mating dramas play such a big part in the sex lives of some birds that the act of fertilization itself becomes almost perfunctory. Nowhere are the rituals preceding courtship more elaborate than with the bowerbirds – a small, ordinary-looking group of birds found only in northern Australia and New Guinea. Bowerbird males seem to take their preparations for courtship more seriously than any other animal, with the possible exception of human beings.

The nineteen different species of bowerbird all prepare for mating by constructing large, elaborately decorated stages or "bowers" made of grasses, twigs and colored materials. These structures are built in various shapes and sizes, depending on the species of bowerbird. Some are open promenades, while others have closed tops, resembling tents or teepees. Some are compact and delicate, while others are quite large. In defiance of expectation, the smallest of all known species, the robin-sized golden bowerbird, builds bowers that tower up to nine feet.

Bowers are built by individual males, who indulge in construction mania for several weeks each year just prior to mating. After completing the basic structure, each male decorates its bower using what appears to be a combination of instinct and individual taste. The walls and ground nearby are laid out with carefully chosen, color-coordinated items gathered from the surrounding countryside. Flowers, shells and the translucent wings of insects are combined with a wide variety of ready-made collectibles (key chains, coins, bullets and in at least one instance a pilfered glass eye). The resulting array is as festive as a folk-art altar. As a finishing touch, some varieties of bowerbird paint the walls of their constructions using leaves for brushes and ground-up berries, charcoal or stolen packets of sky-blue laundry detergent for paint.

The ultimate purpose of these monuments is ostensibly to impress prospective mates. When a suitable female happens along, the male goes into a frantic song-and-dance on and around his colorful temple, singing wildly while picking up and waving his various collected objects. If the female is suitably impressed by the show she will consent to enter the temple of seduction for a quick round of sex. With this out of the way, the usefulness of the bowerbird's great monument is essentially exhausted. The female does not linger but instead flies off to start work on a nest of her own in which she will raise her young without any help from the male.

Left alone with his masterpiece, the male, who mates only once in a season, inexplicably refuses to abandon his work to decay, but returns to the housekeeping routine he had established before the female arrived. Withered flower arrangements are replaced, shiny objects are rearranged to catch the optimum amount of light, fading walls receive fresh coats of paint. With this year's mating successfully accomplished, what is the point of all this continued care and attention to the conjugal nest?

"The best available explanation," writes Hilda Simon, "is that the males enjoy them."

MOTHER NATURE'S
GREATEST HITS
12

ARTISTIC APES

The Plight of the Post-modern Chimp

Opinions differ as to whether the bowerbird can really be said to practice art in the sense that humans do. Though genuinely aesthetic choices may be involved in the bird's selection and arrangement of materials, the activity is still very much bound by instinct. Therefore, it might be more accurate to identify the bird's activities with a less lofty term, such as "decoration."

The only animals that have been observed to create objects that can pass as art, at least to the uninformed viewer, are the apes. Captive chimpanzees and gibbons not only enjoy applying paint to canvas but can become somewhat obsessed with the activity, pondering long over the placement of brush strokes and flying into rages if their materials are taken away from them before they feel their work is finished.

If a session is interrupted and the primate painter is given back his or her materials at a later time, work will resume where it was left off until the painting is completed to the ape's satisfaction. Once the painting ape is happy with the way a piece looks, he or she will refuse to apply any further brush strokes and can become very testy if urged to do so.

One of the stranger similarities between ape and human creativity is the negative effect that rewards have on production. Just as human artists sometimes lose their creative spark when fame and fortune come their way, ape painters will become jaded if their efforts are consistently rewarded by gifts of food from their keepers. Once the connection

between painting and material benefits is made, all the fun seems to go out of the process.

The most successful paintings by apes display a definite sense of balance and composition, but so far no ape has succeeded in making the transition from abstract designs to representational imagery. Humans usually pick up this capacity around the age of four. Rough geometric figures and scrawls are suddenly replaced by shapes that are clearly meant to be symbols of something else: a face, an animal, a house. Despite all the care and concentration they put into their canvases, apes are simply incapable of making this comparatively enormous intellectual leap, which means that in spite of the many things we share in common with animals, we humans can still lay claim to at least a few thoroughly unique abilities.

13

FANCY DANCERS

Chimp Stompers, Badger Shufflers and Other Quick Steppers

"Dance" is another one of those ambiguous words defined in different ways by different people. Many animals, from bugs to birds to antelopes, engage in mating dances of one kind or another, but these are typically very rigid, stereotyped performances involving little in the way of playful improvisation.

What makes human dance so extraordinary is that it is not a strictly programmed impulse alone, but the blending of deeply ingrained "instinctive" rhythmic impulses with individual creative expression and social convention. Rhythm of some kind is common to most forms of human dance, but other than that it is essentially an "open" activity capable of taking on an almost infinite variety of forms. Scholars have theorized that humankind's first dances were developed by our prehistoric ancestors from movements they observed in other animals. Some of the most sophisticated varieties of dance in the world today still bear distant re-semblances to the mating dances of various species of mammal or bird.

Very few animals are capable of making up spontaneous, rhythmic movements that can qualify as dance by human standards, but a handful do. These include chimpanzees, which have been observed swaying and stomping in circles around objects like trees or large rocks. Badgers are another dancing species which, according to Sally Carrighar, perform "a shuffle dance that is very much like the twist."

MASTERS OF MIGRATION

The Salmon, the Eel and the Loneliness of the Long-distance Flapper

One of the supreme riddles of the natural world is that of migration. The figures alone are daunting: Arctic terns cover more than 22,000 miles every year in their seasonal round trips from the Arctic to the Antarctic; salmon make 2,000-mile journeys from the depths of the oceans to the creeks and rivers of their birth; and baby American and European eels traverse 4,000 miles from their birthplace deep in the Sargasso Sea in the Carribean. These well-known feats still boggle the imagination.

Though ancient observers of animals had long suspected it

might exist, the phenomenon of migration was not proved to be a fact until a few hundred years ago. A number of imaginative theories were put forward to account for the seasonal disappearances of certain species of birds before the truth began to emerge piece by piece. One of the most inspired theories was that of the Bishop of Hereford who suggested that they flew to the moon.

Today the routes and destinations of many migratory animals have been closely mapped, but the methods they use to accomplish their journeys are still largely open to question. Smell certainly plays a large part in fish migrations, and birds have been shown to rely at least partially on solar and celestial navigation.

Major movers and shakers

Animal migrations fall into a number of special categories depending on the frequency with which they take place, the purposes for which they are undertaken and whether they involve one-way or round-trip journeys. Lemmings, for example, are not migratory animals in the truest sense of the word because their famous mass eruptions are confused and undirected affairs in which hordes of these tiny, softball-sized rodents move across land and water in many directions at once. Most die nasty deaths of one kind or another along the way, and those that survive generally don't ever see their point of origin again.

More orderly, seasonal migrations are undertaken by representatives of every major animal group. Among the reptiles, the sea turtle makes the most impressive long-term migrations (a standard round trip for a green sea turtle can involve a journey as great as 2,400 miles). Among land mammals, hoofed species such as caribou, reindeer and wildebeest make the most substantial moves. Many whales are also champion migrators, traversing entire oceans in the course of a single year.

A number of insects regularly migrate in huge numbers over enormously long distances without straying from routes followed by their ancestors for thousands, and perhaps millions, of years. The most famous insect migrant may be the monarch butterfly of North America, which not only manages to follow precise travel routes from Canada all the way to central Mexico but also uses exactly the same trees year after year as resting places. The butterfly's evergreen roosts become so thick with orange-and-black wings during winter months that these trees seem to have the shivers.

Among fish, the most skilled migratory navigators are the eel and, of course, the salmon. Individuals of these species somehow manage to find their way back to the exact streams in which they were hatched years before. The greatest authenticated migratory labor ever performed by an animal was probably that of a coho salmon raised in a California fish hatchery and released in a nearby stream. This fish not only made it safely to the Pacific but managed to return as a full-grown adult to the enclosed tank in which it had been raised. The last stretch of this singularly improbable journey required the fish to thread its way through underground drainage ditches and a tortuous stretch of four-inch pipe that twisted at right angles and came to a halt at a wire mesh screen. The salmon broke through this screen and then threaded through a sophisticated netting system designed to keep the

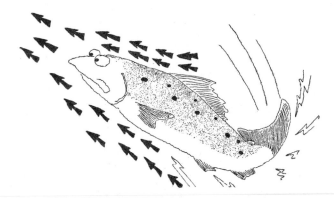

captive salmon on the other side from getting out, and arrived, at last, in the exact enclosure of water in which it had first seen the light of day.

The loneliness of the long-distance flapper

The longest migratory journeys are made by birds. This makes sense, given the fact that their wings allow them to travel through space more efficiently and quickly than other creatures. It is puzzling, however, that the most accomplished migratory birds are often flimsy, lightweight species that wouldn't seem to stand a chance out on the stormy wastes of the open ocean over which many of them routinely travel. The ruby-throated hummingbird weighs less than some insects and can be completely enclosed in the palm of a human hand, yet every year these birds traverse more than 500 miles across the Gulf of Mexico to their wintering grounds in Central America.

The jury is still out on how these extraordinary journeys are accomplished. The surface of the earth is alive with subtle electromagnetic forces which probably play a part in the migratory process. But even if factors like smell, light and magnetic fields are involved, the question of how creatures of limited intelligence manage to make use of such complex information remains a mystery. Accurate solar and celestial navigation is a very complex undertaking, and the idea that birds and fish, much less a brainless bunch of butterflies, possess the capacity to somehow "understand" and act on the data they receive from the outside world does not mesh with most of modern science's assumptions about the capacities of the animal mind.

TIMEKEEPERS

The Punctual Porcupine and Other Internal Clock Punchers

A faculty that scientists now believe to be essential for animal navigation is a highly accurate sense of time. Many animals, most notably bees, somehow seem always to know exactly what time it is in spite of the fact none of them is remotely capable of understanding time itself. (Actually, we humans aren't too sure what it is either, but that's beside the point.)

Animals with a highly developed sense of time are often said to possess an "internal clock" – a phrase that sounds as if the capacity were well understood, which it isn't. This faculty appears not only in migratory animals but in relatively sedentary ones as well, and may play a part in facilitating a number of activities unrelated to travel. Porcupines, for example, don't get around much, but they nevertheless seem to possess a very fine-tuned internal clock. One prickly individual was observed to pass by a particular spot at the same time every evening for seven years. He probably maintained this schedule even longer than that, but the individual who kept track of this feat apparently had to move on to other projects.

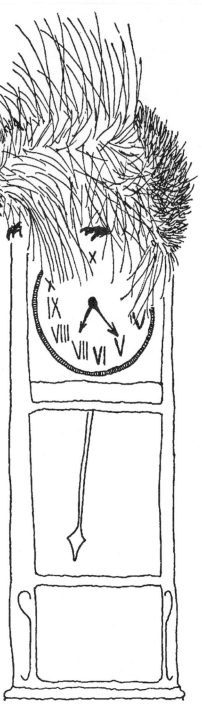

Though it's usually not as sharply tuned as that of many animals, humans have internal clocks of their own. A few years ago an investigator decided to test the reliability of his internal time-sense by spending several months deep in a Texas cave where no hints from the outside world could penetrate to tell him whether it was night or day. He found that his body was, in fact, somehow able to adjust itself and maintain a regular schedule in spite of the absence of all external clues.

SUCCESSFUL CREEPS

The Universal Abundance of Worms

Mother Nature has produced some impressively flashy creatures in the course of the earth's history, but the success and abundance of what science calls "the lower and higher wormlike organisms" shows that she has an equal fondness for life forms distinctly lacking in charm, grace or flair.

Consider the offensively businesslike world of the tapeworm, who spends the entirety of its adult life within the digestive tract of larger, more sophisticated animals, mooching nutrients, laying eggs, and sometimes growing to the alarming length of thirty feet. Or consider the more complex but equally off-putting life cycle of the closely related Chinese liver fluke, which makes its home in the bile duct of the human liver, feeding and laying eggs that pass into the outside world via human feces. In order for these eggs to hatch they must be eaten by a particular species of snail. Within the snail's liver, they develop into larva capable of swimming independently in sea water. Once they "hatch" from the unfortunate snail which has nurtured them, these insidious freeloaders search for a passing fish and burrow into its flesh. There they enter a state of confident torpidity and wait for the fish in question to be caught and consumed by a human, at which point they head for the liver and the whole fiendish process repeats itself.

Creeps of the deep

Elsewhere in the creepy, robotic world of worms are species with heads that repeatedly disintegrate and re-form while their bodies remain intact. There are also worms with no respiratory, digestive or circulatory systems. One recently discovered species can attain lengths up to ten feet and is so single-mindedly primitive it has neither a stomach, a set of eyes, nor even a mouth. Fortunately for the squeamish among us, these creatures exist only in tremendously deep areas of the Pacific Ocean.

As if all this weren't enough, this unappealing class of animals turns out to be the most successful form of multicellular organism in existence – if success is measured by longevity and sheer number of individuals. The longest surviving species of complex organism is something called *Neopelina galatheae,* a deep-ocean wormlike creature which has been on the planet for at least the last 500 million years.

There are approximately 40,000,000,000,000,000,000,000,000 nematode sea worms currently residing in the world's oceans – a considerably greater number than the paltry 5,000,000,000 specimens of homo sapiens now alive. As a final indignity, the lowly worm family turns out to count among its members the longest (if not the bulkiest) of the world's creatures – the ocean-dwelling bootlace worm. This slinky behemoth can grow to lengths of at least 180 feet, far outdistancing both the blue whale and the giant squid.

INSECT HORRIFICS

**Disease, Cannibalism and Other
Unsettling Facts of Bug Life**

Even for those of us who aren't cursed with the strange psychological affliction that causes some people to run screaming at the sight of the tiniest bug, there is something about the insect world that inspires distrust. To begin with, there are infinitely more of them than there are of us, and as a group they have so far shown no inclination to decrease their numbers despite all our efforts to that end. While more and more of Mother Nature's higher species are driven to extinction by human advances, the insects of the world have suffered our rise to power with very few major catastrophes. This is principally because they reproduce so rapidly and in such astronomical numbers that they can adapt to even the most sweeping and abrupt environmental changes. With each successful mating between two different insects come new genetic combinations that allow each species to continually adapt to new environmental dangers, be they natural or engineered by humans. And there are always plenty of mating insects around.

Hoards of staunch resisters

A well-known statistic about the breeding ability of the housefly provides a good illustration of just how little chance human beings, with their arsenal of poisons, stand against an insect opponent. During one summer alone a single pair of houseflies, under ideal conditions, could produce as many as 335,923,200,000,000 offspring.

Houseflies are notorious disease spreaders due to their habit of coughing up small amounts of previously eaten food on each new potential food source they land on. This somewhat repulsive method of feeding (known as the "vomit drop" technique among students of bug behavior) has played a major part over the centuries in distributing a large number of catastrophic human ailments – including cholera, typhoid, leprosy and the plague.

Mosquitos pose an even greater threat as disease carriers and have proven equally impossible to eradicate. The Western

BUGUS CREEPUS

medfly has cheerfully accommodated itself to every new poison custom-made for it, as has the fire ant, a recent invader of the Southern states, which has a habit of jamming up traffic lights and other electronic mechanisms. These and other insect nations continue to take everything we can dole out to them with scarcely a flinch.

Survivors with a vengeance

One reason why human offensives don't seem to impress insects much is that the world was already a diabolically harsh place for them long before we entered the picture. Violence and hardship are inescapable aspects of life for all creatures, but compared to the horrible things that insects regularly do to one another, the brutal indignities that even the fiercest of the higher animals inflict seem benign. Many female insects have a tendency to eat their sexual partners either during or immediately after intercourse. To avoid this, some male spiders actually tie up their chosen mates before proceeding with the business of impregnation. Other male spiders distract their generally much larger feminine partners by "tickling" them in certain areas while hurriedly depositing their sperm with a specialized leg called a "palp."

The raising of the young among the insects can take equally unsettling forms. The practice is given its most horrific twist by those species – especially wasps – that lay their eggs in living victims. When the eggs hatch, the young linger for a while in the flesh of their unwitting host, feeding on it until they are ready to break away and pursue life on their own. If the host animal is a small one (such as another bug), the process of supporting these opportunistic children usually proves fatal.

GREATEST HITS

18

MULTITUDINOUS BEETLES

The Champions of Variation

Anyone who has spent a warm summer evening in a room with one or more June bugs might be surprised to learn that these bouncing, buzzing incompetents are members of the most successful family of animals in the world. June bugs are beetles, and there are more varieties of beetles in existence than there are of any other kind of creature whatsoever...even worms. About 300,000 species have been catalogued so far, but some experts suggest this may be only a fraction of the actual number. The nature writer David Quammen cites one expert who believes the total number of distinct species might run as

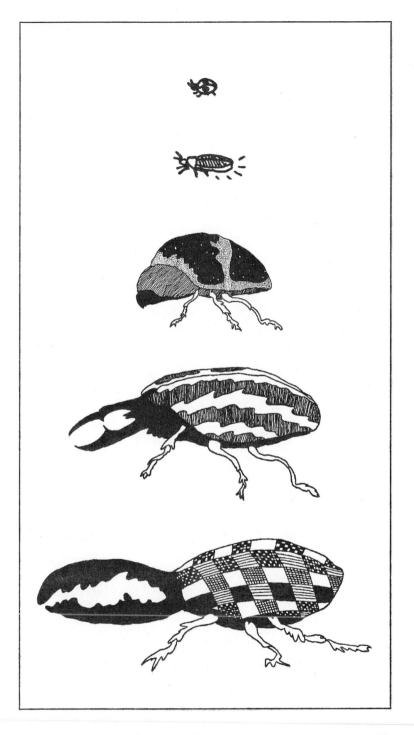

high as twelve million.

Any family this big is bound to contain a considerable amount of variation. Indeed, not all species immediately suggest "beetle" to the untrained observer. In addition to the roundish, shiny-backed, "standard" beetle species there are others which look more like ants or cockroaches, and still others which look like walking Swiss Army knives with the can-opener blade pulled out. Some beetles live underwater and hunt small fish and amphibians. Others burrow through the ground or fly through the air, though usually not with much grace. Two of America's most well-liked insects – the firefly and the ladybug – are beetles. The glow mechanism of the former functions as a device for attracting members of the opposite sex. Some tropical species have developed their radiance to such a degree that it is possible to read a newspaper or find one's way through a dense jungle on a moonless night from the light of a single individual.

The giant of insects

The word's biggest insect is the rotund, clunking Goliath beetle of the jungles of central Africa. It reaches almost six inches in length and can weigh up to four ounces – about two-thirds the weight of this book. Aside from its capacity to shock the timid, the Goliath beetle does not pose a threat to humans. Like the handful of other super-beetles that approach it in size, it is a slow-moving, slightly comical beast that stays to itself when not engaged in mating dramas with other members of its own species.

The males of some giant-size beetles are armored with enormous, multi-pronged "horns" that sometimes make up half the length of their bodies. These devices look incredibly dangerous but aren't. As far as close observers have been able to make out, they are used mostly for hoisting other beetles of the same species up into the air. A pair of stag beetles competing for a mate take turns using their lengthy and cumbersome horns to pick up and drop each other, more or less like a pair of aging wrestlers struggling to please a crowd. Not much harm comes to either beetle from this, but after a time one of them will get fed up and depart, at which point the victor sometimes sweeps up his weighty female prize and clunks away holding her high in his horns.

A compendium of creepy crawlers

For those who find numbers such as 300,000 hard to grasp, here is a sampling of the common names of a few of the 28,600 varieties of beetles found in the continental United States. These examples were lifted at random from the index of Borror and White's *Field Guide to the Insects:*

aberrant long-horned	marsh
ambrosia	may
antlike flower	metallic wood-boring
antlike leaf	minute bog
ant-loving	minute fungus
bark-gnawing	minute marsh
comb-clawed	minute marsh-loving
cucumber	patent leather
death-watch	pill
dry-fungus	pleasing fungus
elephant	powder-post
engraver	rhinoceros
false blister	root-eating
false clown	sap
false tiger	scarab
feather-winged	shining fungus
flea	soldier
flour	spider
flower	stag
fringe-winged	tiger tortoise
handsome fungus	trout-stream
horseshoe crab	tumbling flower
lizard	water penny
long-horned	wedge-shaped
long-horned leaf	whirligig

To Eat or Be Eaten

Insects and worms certainly do not have a monopoly on ruthless, cold-blooded survival strategies. Reptiles, birds and even mammals all have a number of habits that are difficult for the faint-hearted to swallow. The larger mammalian predators often take a long time to kill their victims. The process can be so unsettling, in fact, that the producers of television programs on predatory mammals often censor footage of these beasts devouring their still-conscious, warm-blooded prey.

Many snakes swallow their victims whole while they are still alive. Snake-eating birds like the roadrunner of the American southwest return the favor by gulping down snakes using similarly unpleasant methods. It's not an uncommon sight to see one of these quirky and comical birds running around with several inches of twitching rattlesnake tail dangling out of its bill, waiting its turn to be digested after the front end is finished.

Murderous infants and others

Another spectacle from the world of birds that causes trouble for the over-sensitive observer occurs during the life cycle of the cuckoo. Like some other bird species, cuckoos don't look after their own progeny but leave the task up to other birds. The mother cuckoo finds a promising-looking nest with the eggs of another species already in it and speedily lays her own there while no one is looking. The cuckoo egg tends to hatch before the others, producing a large, naked chick which immediately sets to pushing its foster siblings over the edge. Footage of this process has an eerie, mechanical quality to it. The baby cuckoo obviously has no idea what it is doing but instead is operating on pure instinct, which somehow makes it even harder for us soft-hearted humans to come to terms with it.

Another excessively competitive infant is the baby sand-tiger shark. The young of this species don't wait to be born to commence the shark-eat-shark business of survival but start while still in the mother's womb. Like most sharks, the sand-tiger gives birth to live young, but by the time the hour of birth has arrived only one or two of the creatures emerges into the light of day instead of the dozen or so that most sharks produce. The reason for this is that the less assertive infants have already been devoured while still in the darkness of the mother's belly. Once out in the open, the winners of the competition must hastily depart or they too will be eaten – by their mother.

STARTLING SNAKES

**Springing Vipers and Other
Surprising Serpents**

It's usually the case that those who fear snakes the most know little about their actual habits. This may be just as well in some cases, for it might not be a source of comfort for such people to know that in addition to the usual species that crawl and slither, there is an Asian variety known as the paradise snake that on occasion flattens itself and glides through the air. Also found in Asia are species that spring violently up into the air to capture birds in flight.

Bouncing vipers and deep throats

Other areas for snake-squeamish vacationers to avoid are those portions of South America inhabited by jumping vipers, which can leap up at potential enemies with terrifying speed and accuracy. Africa also boasts a sizeable number of terrifyingly talented snakes. The spitting cobra, for example, can blind an enemy more than twelve feet away with a well-aimed glob of toxic venom. After pondering such creatures, the most snake-squeamish North American might begin to see our own more sluggish species in a more charitable light.

The snakes of the planet's more far-flung areas possess a number of unusual talents, but one thing they are not good at – despite popular lore to the contrary – is swallowing people. Even the largest of snakes, like the pythons of Africa and the anaconda of South America, both of which can surpass lengths of thirty feet, rarely attempt to swallow humans and are not very successful at it when they do. Although there have been a few reports of children and small adults being gobbled up, these big snakes usually don't tackle prey larger than pigs or wild boar.

RESOURCEFUL RODENTS

Rat Intelligence and the Great Cheese Conundrum

Along with snakes, rats are among the most universally detested creatures in the world. Like the cockroach, they have become expert at living cheek-by-jowel with human beings while cleverly learning to avoid their traps. Each year, rats wreak millions of dollars worth of mischief devouring stored foods, tampering with material goods and generally gumming up the wheels of progress with the detritus of their extravagant communal lifestyles.

Nevertheless, for all that we may complain about them, rats

have also contributed more than their share to human knowledge. Millions upon millions of white rats go thanklessly to their deaths each year in the service of medical science. And white-smocked students of animal behavior seem never to tire of dreaming up bizarre methods for testing their intelligence.

Although the behavior of captive animals may be much easier to study than that of their wild relatives, the caged animals' actions are often warped by the frustrations these creatures suffer in an unnatural environment.

Who's got the cheese?

A sizable percentage of experiments conducted by laboratory scientists and their students are often unnecessarily cruel affairs that say more about the stupidity of humans than the intelligence of rats. Yet a few studies have taught us something about how these resourceful creatures go about solving tough logistical problems. Consider, for instance, the

following conundrum described by Jacques Graven in his book, *Non-Human Thought:*

Three rats were trained to the fairly simple task of pressing a lever to obtain a piece of cheese. They were then placed together in a cage where the lever was some distance from the hole out of which the cheese fell.

"At this point," writes Graven, "the situation becomes particularly tense: the rat who works the lever never gets anything as a reward, for the other two who are watching make off with the food before he can get to it.

"During the first day, none of the rats wanted to press the lever, and all three waited desperately in front of the opening, from which of course no food came at all.

"The second day, one of the rats pressed the lever, but only to the advantage of his companions. On the fourth day, one of the animals had a stroke of genius: he quickly pressed the lever three times in a row and, while each of his fellows grabbed one of the balls, he was able to eat the third one at his leisure. Then, he went back to work, and within two hours he had released no less than 1,156 food balls, which allowed all three to glut themselves. His companions, of course, found his good efforts most acceptable: one of them, during all this time, did press the lever three times, but the other did not even deign to touch it."

The only remaining question is – which was the smartest rat?

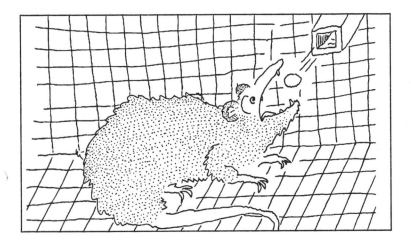

BRAINY BEASTS

Elephant Intelligence, Turkey Stupidity and Other Animal IQs

Only a handful of creatures are equipped with brains larger than those of human beings, and all of these are either dolphins or whales, with one exception: the elephant. Elephants have not received nearly the attention that whales and dolphins have for their super-sized brains, but from the reports of those who have come to know them well, either in captivity or in the wild, it appears that the elephant mind is indeed a subtle and complex one.

Elephants and humans showed up on the planet at roughly the same time – about a million years ago, at the beginning of the most recent ice age. In one way or another, the two species have shared a close relationship ever since. Besides being woolly, the prehistoric mammoth was similar in most other respects to the elephants of today. For thousands of years, various species of woolly mammoths supplied our more enterprising ancestors with a lavish source of food and clothing as well as a supreme test of their hunting skills.

Early human hunting methods were not very sophisticated by today's standards. Perhaps as a result of such sloppy practices as driving entire herds of these creatures off cliffs in order to obtain the meat of only one or two individuals, the world's mammoths became extinct about 10,000 years ago. Two elephant species – the African and Indian – learned to live in the precarious company of homo sapiens well enough to survive to this day, though not without having to endure their share of humiliations and harassments. In addition to killing them for their ivory tusks, we humans have forced elephants to work, to entertain and even to go to war for us.

Elephants for hire

The Indian elephant has been in human employ for more than a thousand years. Yet in spite of all this time, this unique

beast remains less a domesticated animal than a grudging, underpaid accomplice. Indian elephants are exceedingly difficult to train for the same reason they are valued so much as work animals: their big brains. It is fairly easy to get an Indian elephant to master the performance of complex tasks but another thing to keep the pachyderm productive. A captive Indian elephant which develops a "bad attitude" and refuses to continue performing its assigned chores must be isolated immediately or its rebellious spirit will spread to others.

African elephants (which may be on the verge of extinction, thanks to relentless poaching) have the larger brain and are considered to be even more sophisticated in their behavior than their Indian cousins. An African elephant felled by a hunter's bullet will sometimes be helped back to its feet by its companions, which may then stand on either side to help it walk. African elephants not only develop deep and lasting attachments to one another but can even show compassion for other creatures. Rather than trampling a smaller animal too slow or dim-witted to get out of its way, an elephant will sometimes pick it up with its extremely sensitive trunk and place it delicately to one side.

Terrific trunks and terrifying tantrums

Elephants put their trunks to a great variety of uses. Like the human hand, it is a device admirably suited to complement a large and inventive brain. Elephants use their trunks to fill their mouths with the hundred-plus pounds of vegetation they eat daily, and to rocket water down their throats and across their backs at bath-time. Courting elephants use their trunks to rub the bodies of their mates. They will also twine their trunks together in their own version of the human custom of holding hands.

The trunk is also well suited for showing an elephant's displeasure. Overworked Indian elephants have a habit of spraying mud on their owners, and a really irritated pachyderm will pick up and throw rocks or balls of dung. An elephant undergoing a major temper tantrum is one of the more terrifying sights in the natural world. An angry elephant can uproot an entire tree and fling it through the air. If any humans are within reach they may suffer the same treatment.

Stories from the early days of white settlement in India tell of an elephant that was driven to such rage by human encroachment that it began catching and pinning men to the ground, plucking off their arms and legs and flinging them through the air. One can only imagine what kind of cruel behavior the humans in question must have committed to incur such punishment.

Burial of the Dead

Another practice that supposedly sets humans off from animals is our predilection for burying our dead. Though we certainly are a lot more imaginative at it than animals are, we aren't the only creatures who feel the need to lay the bodies of our loved ones to rest in an orderly, respectful fashion. It takes a lot of work to bury an elephant – even for another elephant – but they sometimes go to the trouble anyway.

Badgers, too, will sometimes take great pains to inter the bodies of their fellows, and the roundish graves they occasionally create have been mistaken for human constructions. Though most stories of animal "graveyards" have resulted from a misinterpretation of misleading evidence (such as when a river washes large amounts of animal bones together at a certain spot), some animals do make use of collective resting places. Sick penguins in the Antarctic sometimes wander off and place themselves in voluntary cold storage at the bottom of landlocked bodies of water. One surprised scientist discovered one of these pools and saw what looked like hundreds of perfectly preserved penguins lying at the bottom.

Frozen turkeys and ostrich shepherds

The brains of our feathered earthmates can attain surprising heights of intelligence, a fact to which parrots and mynahs can cheerfully attest. But in some species, animal IQ sinks to equally impressive depths of stupidity, as well. According to Gerald L. Wood, the "least intelligent living bird" is the turkey – more specifically the domesticated variety that appears on tables at Thanksgiving. Whatever wit this creature once possessed in the wild has been completely drained from it by the uneventful centuries it has spent in the care of humans, to the point where it is now so dumb it literally forgets to come in out of the rain.

"Each year," writes Wood, "thousands of turkeys freeze to death on cold nights because they stubbornly refuse to seek refuge in their warm sleeping quarters, and some turkeys are so dim they have to be persuaded to eat."

Among wild birds, ostriches are often singled out for their stupidity, but this reputation seems to have been forced upon them simply because they look funny. Though the ostrich is no genius, it is smart enough to learn how to herd sheep, and in southwest Africa ostriches are somtimes used for just that purpose.

COMPASSIONATE CREATURES

Charitable Crows and
Other Good Samaritans

Charity – the selfless impulse to come to the aid of another creature in distress – is regarded as one of the noblest attributes known to human beings. It is considered to be one of those "higher" traits that gives people a sense of superiority over the rest of the animal kingdom. The idea that a wild animal might be capable of coming to the aid of another – especially one which is not its offspring and perhaps not even of the same species – might seem far-fetched. But there are enough reliable examples of such behavior on record to suggest that the natural world is not always the relentlessly dog-eat-dog place it's been made out to be.

In order for an animal's actions to qualify as genuinely charitable, the behavior needs to be so far outside that creature's normal range of habits that there is no question of misplaced instinct. For example, adult birds of various species have often been observed giving food to chicks that are not their own. In one case, a cardinal was seen stuffing food into the mouth of a goldfish, which popped its head out of its lily pond to make the task easier. Rather than charity, this unusual activity could be more accurately explained as a case of misplaced instinctive parenting (See Number 26).

Famous animal rescues

Less easy to explain is the behavior sometimes shown by sparrows when one of their fellows gets wedged in a hole or snags its claw on a telephone wire. On more than one occasion, observers have watched as the trapped bird is yanked free by its companions. A witness of one such rescue operation reported that the trapped bird was pulled free by not one but two birds, the second one yanking on the tail feathers of the first.

Charitable behavior might also explain an incident in which a seagull was seen choking on something it had swallowed – probably a fish bone. Its fellow gulls gathered around and, after some hesitation, one of them actually reached into the bird's throat and yanked the object free.

An even more remarkable rescue operation was performed by a pet South African crow. According to the couple who

owned it, this crow was on excellent terms with their puppy, who one day disappeared and was not seen for several days. Maurice Burton, in his book *Just Like an Animal*, describes what happened next: "The couple noticed the crow was not eating as usual. It would take some food, fly off, return again and fly off with more food. In the end they followed the crow, which in this way led them to their puppy which was trapped in a snare and for six days had been fed by the crow. The puppy was in perfect condition."

Acts of kindness may be found even among the most unlikely species. Rats have been observed guiding their blind fellow rats. Fish sometimes practice the same behavior when they swim alongside their blind companions and give them occasional bumps to steer them in the right direction.

AMOROUS ANIMALS

Romantic Gorillas and Monogamous Fish

Separating love from less lofty impulses like sex or instinctual attachment is as difficult to do with animals as it is with humans. In more innocent times it was a common practice for nature enthusiasts to see love at work everywhere in the wild – a mother duck distracting a fox from her ducklings by limping and flapping her wings as if wounded, or a Canada goose refusing to abandon the lifeless body of its mate. These and other similar actions were seen as proofs that animals were capable of pure and selfless devotion as noble as that of any human. About a hundred years ago, opinion on the matter was pretty much divided into two camps: those who saw animals as essentially humane beings possessed of noble emotions and heroic qualities, and those who saw all of nature as an ingeniously constructed but essentially soulless machine full of various smaller, furred or feathered machines that acted the way they did because of a mysterious thing called instinct.

Whatever love is, it certainly isn't present everywhere in nature. Most of the "noble," "selfless" actions that so stirred the romantic imaginations of nineteenth-century naturalists are now understood to be innate responses performed automatically by animals under certain conditions. Mother ducks don't really think about luring foxes away from their babies; they do it instinctively. Much the same can be said for many of the other heroic feats performed by animals in the wild.

But this does not mean, as the more mechanistically minded students of animal behavior would still have us believe, that animals are nothing but instinct-driven robots. Animals do, on occasion, act in ways that are very far from automatic and can only be explained when we grant them at least a small measure of "higher order" intelligence. Caught up as they are in the pull of countless instinctive drives, virtually blind to the world of abstract concepts and subtle meanings in which we humans alone are truly at home, many animals seem to indicate nevertheless that they, too, can suffer from that mysterious affliction known as love.

Romantic apes, monogamous fish

Among humans, the two most widely celebrated love relationships are those which develop between parent and child, and so-called "romantic" love. Both varieties are present in the animal world and can reach surprising levels of intensity in some species. Skeptics hold that the "love" that animals show for their children, and vice versa, can generally be chalked up to "blind instinct." But it's not as easy for these nay-sayers to explain away the more inspired animal practitioners of "romantic" love. Several of the more intelligent apes – particularly gibbons and gorillas – are so consistently demonstrative of their affection for their mates that they make humans look somewhat cold by comparison. Dolphins and whales also show devotion for each other that goes far beyond what would be necessary to ensure survival. Captive dolphins who have lost their mates sometimes develop crippling depressions that can lead to illness and even death.

Most people know that certain species of geese are monogamous, but so are wolves, coyotes, foxes, beavers and even a few species of fish. We automatically tend to admire monogamous animals (possibly because of our own difficulties in attaining this state ourselves), but it still remains a matter of opinion as to where instinct ends and "true love" begins.

MOTHER NATURE'S GREATEST HITS

25

PHENOMENAL FRIENDSHIPS

Polar Bears, Arctic Foxes and Other Unlikely Pals

Whether or not one chooses to grant animals the ability to love as humans do, there is no question about their ability to cultivate genuine – and sometimes very unlikely – friendships that have nothing to do with simple "instinctive" drives. Consider for example the

many cases of inter-species friendship that have been observed in domesticated animals. In addition to the case of the African crow and the puppy described in Number 23, there are records of friendships between such seemingly incompatible creatures as goats and rabbits, dogs and horses, and even cats and mice. When such friendships are broken by the death or disappearance of one of the animals, the other one may cease eating and, like the love-sick dolphins mentioned in the last section, actually die of grief.

In the wild, genuine friendships can arise between the most theoretically ferocious animals. Polar bears are often followed around by Arctic foxes which eat the scraps left over from their kills. The bear not only tolerates the fox in situations like this but, according to some observers, actually enjoys the fox's company. Badgers are extremely powerful and feisty animals capable of out-fighting entire packs of dogs, yet under the right circumstances they will strike up friendships with foxes and coyotes and even share their burrows with them. In the nineteenth century, a Canadian badger befriended and looked after a lost boy for more than two weeks, allowing the child to sleep in its den and even bringing him food. Since the badger reaped no material reward for its efforts, it's not unreasonable to suppose that the badger came to the boy's rescue because it was in the mood for companionship.

Pet trout, lobster dinners and devoted dolphins

The capacity for friendship isn't confined to large-brained, warm-blooded animals. With enough patience, certain kinds of fish can learn to recognize and respond to their human owners with genuine enthusiasm. In one verified case, a pet trout was so devoted to its owner that it would slide up onto the bank of the stream where it lived and allow itself to be petted. Human inhabitants of certain South Pacific islands have even succeeded in befriending nurse sharks. And in the Bahamas, a well-known stretch of shallow water is occupied by a group of Atlantic stingrays which flop up like excited puppies onto the heads and shoulders of divers who bring them handouts.

Descending lower still on the evolutionary ladder, there's the case of the lobster who reportedly learned to recognize its master and raise one of its claws up out of its tank at feeding time to receive its dinner. While it might be stretching things to suggest that trout or lobsters are capable of actual affection, the fact that these individual creatures each learned to associate a particular person with its feeding time shows that even the most seemingly primitive animals are capable of relating to humans.

The wild animal best known for its habit of striking up friendships with people is the dolphin. Though they may not carry lost mariners to shore on their backs as often as legend has suggested, dolphins are among the few animals which need no enticement to approach and interact with humans in the wild. Whole pods of these creatures have been known to visit bathing beaches, and individual dolphins have sometimes visited the same beach repeatedly to play with certain humans whom they have come to recognize. Other lone dolphins have taken it upon themselves to linger in particularly dangerous stretches of ocean in order to guide ships safely through them. Though some half-hearted attempts have been made at dismissing these ship-guiding dolphins as victims of misplaced instinct, the truth of the matter seems to be that they are simply well-disposed toward humans and enjoy helping them.

ODD ATTACHMENTS

Misplaced Mother Love and Other Quirky Bonds

"Misplaced mother love" is a term used to describe occasions in which a female of one species takes to mothering the young of an entirely different species. This situation arises quite frequently in nature and can occur between animals that look and act nothing like one another. Cats raising hedgehogs, dogs raising pigs – the list of such unusual relationships is a long one. A captive dolphin once took to mothering a small shark that lived in its tank and almost killed the creature with kindness before aquarium personnel came to the rescue. Baby dolphins need to be taught to come to the surface to breathe, and this misguided dolphin became upset at its foster child's proclivity for the bottom of the tank. The dolphin repeatedly swam down to the baby shark's "rescue," seizing it in her mouth and carrying it up to the surface, where she bumped and nudged the hapless creature along like a rubber ball.

The most famous examples of misplaced mother love are those which take place between wild animals and lost children. Stories of "wolf children" come from all over the world, and many such tales are based on actual occurrences. Bears, gazelles and pigs have also at times taken on the task of raising and educating human children. When such individuals are captured and dragged back to civilization, the re-education process can be long and difficult, and in some cases it fails completely.

Cases of mistaken identity

In the wild, animals of one species occasionally meet and mate with animals of another. But such occurrences are rare and only take place between species that are very closely related (like wolves and coyotes or different kinds of insects, for example). But sex aside, "love" relationships can spring up between species that have nothing in common whatsoever. These situations usually arise when a young animal is raised in the company of other animals of a different species. If it is adopted early enough, the animal will start to think of itself as one of the animals that have taken it in, no matter how great the physical dissimilarity between the species might be.

Konrad Lorenz discovered that animals of various species

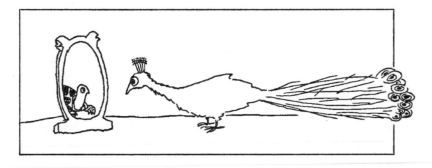

instinctively form bonds with the first creatures they see when they are born. Lorenz called this phenomenon "imprinting" and successfully demonstrated it with several varieties of birds. There is a famous series of photographs showing Lorenz being followed around by a gaggle of greylag geese which had come to think of him as their mother. He also succeeded in developing a "love relationship," of sorts, with a male jackdaw (a member of the crow family) which tried to win his favor by stuffing minced worm bits into his mouth. When Lorenz tired of accepting these gifts and kept his mouth firmly shut, the frustrated suitor shoved worms into his ear. Another well-known case of misplaced romantic love concerned a peacock that had been raised among tortoises. Throughout its adult life it refused to pay any attention to females of its own species and would only display its fan of tail feathers to "other" tortoises.

Sometimes the object of affection can be an inanimate object, such as the case of the goose that developed a crush on a wheelbarrow, as described by Maurice Burton in his book *Just Like an Animal:*

"Except when grazing," writes Burton, "she spent all her time sitting beside it. Anyone approaching the wheelbarrow was treated to an aggressive display, as the goose would have done had she had her partner with her. The goose 'talked' to the wheelbarrow before going off to graze. When someone took the wheelbarrow away, in the normal course of using it, the goose would follow honking and hissing, until the wheelbarrow was left stationary. There were occasions when the wheelbarrow had to be taken well away, out of sight of the goose. Then she would seek the company of the rear wheel of the car parked near the house."

27

SIX-LEGGED SOLDIERS

War and Slavery Among Ants

The non-human world may abound with creatures that can suffer deep emotional attachments, play games and practical jokes on one another, solve difficult logistical problems and invent novel and sometimes ridiculous behaviors just for the fun of it. A few creatures may even approach the periphery of abstract thought. But practically nothing else on earth practices the art of war as humans do. Ants make war with one another for some of the same reasons people do (such as competition for food and territory), but how they manage to engage in an activity as complex as warfare without the benefit of actual brains, no one can explain.

Despite the vast evolutionary distance that separates us from them, ants share a number of other inexplicable and sometimes unsettling habits in common with humans. In their own peculiar way, they resemble us more than any other animal. Substance abuse is one shared habit (as will be described in Number 28). Even more disturbingly humanlike activities practiced by ants include slavery and general mayhem.

Though most ants are tireless, highly skilled workers, several mean-spirited, lazy species survive solely by capturing and enslaving other ants. Some of these slave-keeping species are so specialized that they have lost the ability to do any kind of real work whatsoever. Their massive jaws are good only for slicing up belligerent captive ants. Without a slave population to collect food and feed it to them, they soon starve to death.

Calling out the troops

No creature – other than the human being – is as effective at shaking up life for other animals as the army ant. These carnivorous nomads swarm across the jungles of Africa and tropical America in groups that can stretch for a quarter of a mile or more. Like most ants, they are excellent strategists and somehow manage to coordinate their movements so that a colony of perhaps a million individuals acts as a single unit. Advancing army ants can cross small rivers by forming themselves into living bridges and rafts. If confronted by a wall of fire, those at the head of a procession will throw themselves into it, smothering the flames so that those behind them can proceed. The dim, crunching sound of an army of these creatures on the march is enough to empty

entire forests. Other animals, both large and small, that don't clear out fast enough are either devoured or taken prisoner to be consumed later.

Yet for all the terror they inspire, army ants do have a saving grace of sorts. Traditional healers both in America and Africa have long used them as ready-made stitches for serious wounds. A number of ants are collected and held, one after another, over the wound that needs stitching. As the ant clamps its jaws down, it staples the skin together. The skilled surgeon then swiftly decapitates the ant before it has a chance to release its grip.

As hard as they may be on their neighbors, the biggest victim of the ants' tough, no-nonsense lifestyle is the male ant himself. At some point in their evolution, female ants began taking responsibility for all of the really important tasks at hand, while males became increasingly obsolete to the point where they were only necessary for the production of sperm. As a result, male ants today are treated more or less as disposable reproduction units by the females, who raise them solely for that purpose and devour them immediately afterwards.

Down on the ant farm

Domestication of other species is one skill that ants and humans have in common. Some species of ants have developed astonishingly effective methods of storing and even "farming" food inside their colonies. In addition to tending subterranean fungus gardens, some species actually keep "herds" of other insects (usually aphids) which they protect, feed and "milk" much as humans do with cows or goats. In some cases the aphid herds are housed in separate dwellings built specifically for them by their ant masters who pack away their charges for the night and carry them out in the daytime to graze.

28

TIPSY CRITTERS

Boozing Raccoons, Hung-over Hornets and Other Substance Abusers

"Survival of the fittest," "eat or be eaten." The struggle to maintain one's place in the food chain is a constant preoccupation for creatures large and small, or so most of us have been led to believe. Attending to the business of survival may be the rule of the jungle – and of the backyard lot, for that matter – but this doesn't mean our fellow creatures don't relish the opportunity to take a break from their day-to-day routines just as people do.

Human beings have been enlisting the services of alcohol to break out of their workaday ruts for thousands of years. Its benefits and drawbacks are well-known throughout the world. Where the use of alcohol is suppressed, other intoxicants almost always appear to take its place. It might seem that the tendency to seek out and consume funny-tasting substances is a strictly human habit. Not so. Many animals and even some bugs will gulp down alcohol, gobble up fermented fruit or nibble on intoxicating plants whenever they get the chance.

Bears and their close relative the raccoon share a fondness for fermented berries. Raccoons have been known to use their nimble black fingers to pop open unguarded cans of beer. The scent of leaves from the

catnip plant will attract about fifty percent of all cats and turn them tipsy. And laboratory rats presented with morphine-dispensing devices that operate at the push of a lever quickly turn into junkies (a dependency aided, most probably, by the boredom they suffer in this unnatural environment).

Even such obsessively business-minded creatures as ants and wasps will drop what they are doing if presented with a ready supply of alcohol or some other intoxicating substance. Hornets are among the worst offenders, according to Sally Carrighar in her book, *Wild Heritage:*

"Hornets are fond of alcohol," writes Carrighar, "and if they can get it, usually from fermenting fruit, they become real drunks. They sip it until they fall into a stupor, and when they awake are so thirsty for more that they can't even be bothered to find the nest of another wasp in which to deposit their eggs."

One ingenious bug – the rove beetle – has developed the ability to secrete an intoxicating substance from its own body. Like a number of beetle species, the rove makes its home within the colonies of certain types of ants. The presence of one of these walking stills can reek havoc on the whole colony. Worker ants start hanging out around the beetle, taking occasional licks from its abdomen instead of tending to their normal responsibilities. Soon all structure and purpose is forgotten and the whole colony falls into ruin.

29

BEASTLY BRUTES

Lazy Lions, Degenerate Ducks and Other Lascivious Fiends

In addition to alcoholism, drug abuse, warfare and slavery, some animals also succumb, at times, to a number of other reprehensible human-like habits. It may seem anthropomorphic to accuse lions of being lazy, but there is really no better word to describe their lifestyle, at least for the male of the species. Male lions are chronic loungers. If given the choice, they will sleep or doze for up to twenty out of every twenty-four hours, relying on females to do all the work of securing food and raising the young. If a male lion awakes from one of its interminable naps with a big appetite and no readily available food, it will sometimes devour one of its own cubs rather than expend the effort to go in search of more legitimate game.

In addition to their habitual napping, male lions are also promiscuous. They while away many of their few waking hours in leisurely copulation with any available females which will tolerate their advances.

Sloths are often accused of laziness, too. It is true that they are incredibly sluggish creatures, moving so slowly and so infrequently that vegetation takes root in their fur. However, this is more a result of their extremely slow metabolisms than of willful lethargy.

Behaviors that, in humans, would be considered sexually degenerate are more widespread in the animal world than many people realize. "Wife-beating" and rape are common in some (but by no means all) species of apes. Female chimpanzees will submit to sex when not in season if a male bullies them enough. They will also sometimes practice a rudimentary form of prostitution by submitting to males in exchange for food or protection.

Rape is also an ugly reality for – of all creatures – ducks. Ruthless gangs of male pintail ducks have been observed attacking a single female. Scientists have thus far failed to provide a reasonable biological explanation for this strange form of bird brutality.

FEARLESS MARINERS

The Weird, Whiskered Catfish

More than 2,000 species of catfish are at large in the world today, most of them carrying the familiar assemblage of whisker-like barbels that inspired their name. Catfish never have scales, but they can have almost anything else – from toxic venom to potent electrical charges to lunglike organs that allow them to flop out of water for lengthy sojourns on land. Most of the more unusual species have names that refer to their particular talents. Walking catfish have a fondness for walking on land and do so frequently. Climbing catfish like to climb steep rocky cliffs. Upside down catfish enjoy swimming upside down. Talking catfish make grunting sounds by rubbing their pectoral bones together. There are catfish that are long and skinny and look like eels and sluggish, bottom-dwelling species that look like old, discarded shoes. The giant catfish of European waters can grow to lengths of fourteen feet and has been said to suck down human beings on occasion. In former days, when a villager wanted to procure one of these fishes for the lavish supply of meat it provided, he would bait an enormous hook and haul the creature out of the water with the aid of a pair of oxen or horses.

A tiny monster of the deep

Opinions differ, but some say the most fearsome fish in all the waters of the world is a miniscule South American parasitic catfish called a candiru. For reasons not yet entirely understood, these slender little fish have a habit of darting up the urinary tracts of human beings who swim or wade through rivers and streams. A really willful candiru can penetrate as far upstream as the bladder, but even if it doesn't get this far, extrication is usually impossible without surgery.

HYPERACTIVE GLUTTONS

The Ravenous World of the Ancient, Ever-eating Shrew

The expression "we come from fish" is familiar to most veterans of high-school biology classes, but the statement "we come from shrews" has somehow never caught on, despite the fact that it is just as valid.

The 260-odd species of shrews now alive on the planet are the oldest true mammals still in existence ("true" meaning that they don't lay eggs, and nourish their young in the womb by means of a placenta). The original shrewlike ancestors of all true mammals – including humans – which scurried around for millions of years beneath the feet of the dinosaurs, were most

97

likely almost identical to those which continue to scurry around beneath our feet today. In many parts of the world the shrew is still the most numerous mammal per acre of wild land, and most of the backyards of North America are full of them. Despite the fact that they occur in enormous numbers on every continent except Australia, shrews are rarely seen in the wild. This is because they are nocturnal and secretive by nature and move so fast that they are hard to glimpse, even on those rare occasions when they venture out into the open. Shrews are also quite small, with the average pygmy shrew weighing in at less than one U.S. dime.

Eating their way through life

Natural history writers love to describe shrews as the "bloodthirstiest" animals in the world because of the astounding number of bugs, worms, fish, mice, rabbits and other creatures they burn through in the course of their fast and furious lives. The question of whether they really are bloodthirsty depends on how one defines the term, however. If this description is taken to mean a desire to kill for killing's sake instead of simply to secure food, then shrews are not even in the running, since they eat everything they kill.

Because they need to eat at least their weight in high-protein food every day to support their super-fast metabolisms (only that of the hummingbird is faster), shrews spend virtually every waking moment furiously searching for other creatures to devour and will tackle quarry many times larger than themselves. A single hour without food will drive a shrew into a literal frenzy of hunger, and if two or more of these creatures are confined without other available fare, the hungriest will eat the others and finally itself, starting from its tail and moving up from there.

Despite the incredible longevity of shrews as a species, individuals rarely survive for more than a few months in the wild. Their days are too packed with violence for them to avoid death for very long, either at the hands of predators like owls, other shrews or potential prey large enough to successfully fight back. Their lives are so full of stress and they constantly live at such a frenzied pitch that they can even succumb to heart attacks.

Leaving a bad taste in the mouths of their enemies

To aid these intrepid creatures in their perpetual struggle to fill and refill their tiny gullets, Mother Nature has provided them with a number of built-in advantages. Most species possess potent musk glands that make them smell and taste terrible, so that the more discerning larger predators avoid eating them unless they're really desperate. A few species also possess a venomous bite capable of paralyzing smaller animals and causing a good deal of pain to larger creatures like coyotes and curious nature enthusiasts.

Venomous or not, shrews do not hesitate to sink their sharp little fangs into any animal or human that backs them into a situation where escape is no longer possible. Many naturalists attempting to capture these creatures in the wild have been impressed by their fearless behavior. In a *Scientific American* article, Oliver Pearson reported that individuals of a particular

American species "when cornered, throw their heads back, open their mouths and utter a long, shrill chatter that sounds like the song of the Tennessee warbler."

Mighty mites

Of all obstacles that stand before these ever-hungry, miniscule animals, the greatest is that many species have dismally poor eyesight. These nearly blind shrews find their way around their chosen hunting territories largely by memory, sticking to rigidly established trails and straying from them only when necessary. They locate prey by means of smell and touch and, in some species at least, by making constant high-pitched squeaks which they use as an echolocation system much like that of bats, though less sophisticated.

The mole and his holes

It seems unfair to spend so much time on the shrew without at least mentioning its closest living relative, the mole. The life of the mole is not nearly as full of intrigue and bloodshed as that of its voracious cousin. The mole's primary food consists of worms, which it hunts in a comparatively leisurely manner by circulating through the underground mazes that golf enthusiasts and gardeners find so infuriating.

Like the shrew, the mole keeps out of sight as much as possible and will not linger in the open air if any diggable soil is available. Moles are extremely accomplished diggers. One of these creatures placed on reasonably soft ground can bury itself completely in less than a second. They are so partial to digging, in fact, they sometimes do it in their sleep.

MOTHER NATURE'S GREATEST HITS

32

MYTHICAL MONSTERS

Ogopongo, Slimy Slim and Other Denizens of the Deep

The inky lochs of Scotland are by no means the only landlocked bodies of fresh water purported to harbor huge, slimy, humpbacked survivors from the age of the dinosaurs. Russia appears to have a fair number of them as well, as does Sweden, where late last century several attempts were mounted to harpoon one of the creatures and bring it to scientific justice.

Whenever the Native Americans of Lake Okanagan in British Columbia went hunting or fishing on certain parts of the lake's surface, they traditionally offered sacrifices to a beast they knew

as Naitaka. The creature was later renamed Ogopongo by a party of astonished whites who also witnessed it surfacing on occasion. This animal is but one of several Canadian lake beasts that have been reported up to the present day. Others include Manipogo of Lake Winnipegosis in Manitoba and Igopogo of Lake Simco, just forty minutes outside of Toronto. The United States has a less impressive roster, with Slimy Slim of Lake Payette, Idaho, being perhaps the most famous example.

Though all attempts to photograph one of these animals close up have so far met with about as much success as the Swedes' attempts to harpoon one, this might be due to their reclusive habits rather than their nonexistence. Lake monsters are said to favor very deep bodies of water, presumably making a good enough living at the bottom that they only need to come up to the surface for an occasional gulp of air. The most reliable sightings suggest that if and when Slimy Slim or one of its Canadian or European cousins is apprehended, it will be anywhere from thirty to seventy feet in length with a humped back, a graceful, snakey neck terminating in a head resembling a dog's or a sheep's and four paddle-like legs suitable for underwater lake travel. Reports of these creatures sloshing up onto dry land to graze on trees, animals and small children are undoubtedly greatly exaggerated.

MOTHER NATURE'S GREATEST HITS

33

TENTACULAR GIANTS

Flotsam and Jetsam from the World of the Giant Squid

The kraken, or giant squid, is an animal seemingly custom-made for collectors of sensationalistic nature lore. Whatever angle one chooses to take, strange and outlandish facts and stories readily present themselves. In addition to being the largest invertebrate creature alive on earth, with verified lengths of fifty feet and reported lengths of more than twice that, the giant squid sports a pair of the world's largest eyeballs, with specimens recorded of over fifteen inches in diameter. Deep water creatures by nature, giant squids occasionally jet up to the surface of the world's oceans where, lolling along slowly, they have frequently been mistaken for half-sunken ships.

Encounters between giant squids and humans are rare but almost always violent affairs, usually because the homo sapiens in question tend to poke, shoot, harpoon or otherwise molest these creatures instead of simply observing them. Maritime history is full of tales of giant squids plucking seamen from the rigging of ships and devouring them with their enormous, bird-like beaks. Giant squids have even been accused of pulling entire ships beneath the waves. In reality, in all authenticated tussles between human beings and these tentacled opponents, it is the latter who have gotten the worst of it.

Surely the silliest squid "attack" in recent times was that which occurred on the Isle of Skye in 1952. A policeman was patrolling a beach in the aftermath of a powerful storm when he came upon a suspicious lump of flesh protruding from the sand. Showing his species' customary sensitivity for the new and the unknown, he gave the lump a swift kick with his boot. The lump immediately came to life, wrapping a long, tentacled arm around the officer's boot and holding on to it so stubbornly that in the end the officer had to leave it behind, fleeing half-barefoot up the beach. The boot was later recovered and the unfortunate animal dispatched with an axe. The sea creature measured just under nine feet long, making it a comparative runt by giant squid standards.

OMNIVOROUS JAWS

Boat Cushions, Beer Bottles and Other Secrets of the Shark's Stomach

Though they may not look it, sharks are in their own way very sensitive creatures. They can smell blood dissolved in water at less than one part per million, sense the electro-magnetic vibrations created by a fish or wounded animal, and even possess comparatively good eyesight.

Yet, in spite of all this sophisticated equipment, they are incredibly undiscerning eaters. A number of species will swallow just about anything they can get their jaws around. The habit generally doesn't do them much harm because the lining

of the shark's stomach is extremely resilient. Anything that isn't digestible is kept inside for a while and then vomited back up – sometimes along with the animal's entire stomach. When the undigestibles have been disposed of, the stomach is gulped back down and the shark returns to the all-consuming task of filling it up again.

Some items reportedly taken from the stomachs of sharks over the years include the following:

Beer cans, full and empty
A headless knight in armor
A horse (whole)
A reindeer (almost whole)
A buffalo skin
Nine assorted shoes (in a single shark)
Automobile tires
Automobile license plates
A spaniel (whole)
A yellow-bellied cuckoo
25 bottles of Vichy water (in a single shark)
Boat cushions
A crocodile's head
A can of salmon (unopened)
Two pounds of rolled copper wire

As the oceans are filled with more and more garbage, sharks encounter more and more bizarre items and always try to swallow them – sometimes with disastrous results. A shark turned up in Cuba several decades ago with an automobile tire not in its stomach but around it. It's been suggested that the shark was charging through a mass of assorted junk dumped from a boat or barge and had the misfortune to accidentally swim straight through the center of the tire and get caught.

SAVVY SURVIVORS

The Determined Beaver and Other Persistent Creatures

Beavers are such thoroughly curious creatures that they have received an especially generous amount of attention by collectors of nature lore. It's fairly common knowledge that this largest of North American rodents cuts down trees with its teeth to build extensive dams and communal lodges, and that the beaver's gift for construction makes it second only to the human species in its impact on the natural environment.

One beaver fact that might not be as well-known is this animal's tremendous stubbornness in choosing and sticking to a dam site. Once a family of beavers has arrived at a choice location for a dam and set to work building it, nothing short of kidnapping or murder will prevent the group from seeing its project through. Jean Craighead George, in her book *Beastly Inventions*, describes a futile struggle waged by a group of scientists from the Rocky Mountain Biological Station to persuade a determined family of Colorado beavers to shift the location of a dam that was causing flooding on a nearby road. Each time the beavers' dam was laboriously dismantled by the scientists, it was replaced overnight by an even larger one. After several days of this, the biologists' patience ran out and they decided to box-trap the animals and ship them off to another wilderness area. The traps were accordingly set and "by dawn the treadles had been sprung by sticks and the boxes were part of the dam."

Staying power

This same spirit of dogged defiance in the face of human encroachment has been shown by many another harassed species. In most such encounters, the humans in question were not quite as civilized and forgiving as were the Colorado

biologists. Yet, despite guns, traps and bulldozers, some wild creatures have still managed to stand up to humankind and all of the underhanded strategies it has used to drive animals, such as the beaver, from their rightful domains.

Considering the amount of effort that has been put into killing coyotes over the past few hundred years, it is nothing short of a miracle that these wild creatures still roam free in America. The coyote has been trapped, poisoned, burned, shot at and generally harassed more than any other American animal, yet it continues to inhabit much of its original territory and has even managed to move into new areas. The constant challenge of dealing with human aggression has sharpened the coyote's wits to such an extent that the contemporary coyote is probably even more intelligent than its forebears, which Native Americans celebrated as the wisest of animals.

Hunting dogs are generally no match for coyotes, and whole packs of dogs have been made to look foolish by the tricks their clever cousins love to play on them. A favorite ploy of coyotes pursued by dogs is for two individuals to take turns running the pack. While one coyote rests in an out-of-the-way spot, his partner leads the dogs in circles until he is close to exhaustion. The well-rested partner then takes the first one's place and continues to lead the dogs in further circles, the process continuing until the dogs can take no more and are forced to give up in disgust.

The wily raccoon and the defiant wolf

Similar techniques are employed by another great American survivor: the raccoon. These intelligent and engaging offshoots of the bear clan have been given almost as bad a time by humans as the coyote. Yet they, too, manage to survive and sometimes to flourish, even in areas where the human population is extremely dense. Raccoons are good swimmers and have been known to deliberately lead hunting dogs out onto open bodies of water. Once the raccoon has lured its pursuers far from shore, it doubles back and clambers on top of the dogs' heads until they either drown or learn their lesson and head back.

In case you wondered, the nickname of "lone wolf" didn't come about by accident. Although the North American wolf has all but lost the battle today, it held its own on this continent against all odds for an impressively long time, given the campaign of extermination that was waged against it. While these animals were largely extinct in North America by the mid-1800s, renegade wolves continued to persist up into the early years of this century in a number of Western states. Wise to the workings of guns and even the most ingeniously set traps, these individuals drifted from county to county, causing mayhem by killing large numbers of sheep and cattle and leaving them to rot. This kind of indiscriminate destruction is contrary to the normal ways of wolves. The best ex- planation for it is that these determined survivors were giving a last, defiant show of contempt for the forces that had stolen their world from them.

MOTHER NATURE'S
GREATEST HITS
36

SERENE SWIMMERS

The Good Life of Sea Mammals

Around seventy million years ago a group of smallish, carnivorous, piglike animals came to the conclusion that the ages-long struggle for life on dry land had been something of a waste of time. Like someone who, on the way to the shower, suddenly remembers it's Saturday morning and heads back for the comfort of bed, this little-understood group of animals waded back into the waters, let their hooves turn back into fins, and said goodbye forever to the cares and troubles of life on land.

In many ways, the move was a shrewd one, for if life is best where the work is least, then the ocean is a far better place to be than dry land. Free from the constraints of gravity and with plenty of easily available, nutritious food, these rebellious sea pigs gradually reassumed the general shape of their fishy ancestors while retaining the lungs they had developed in order to live on land. Over the eons, the bodies of some of these creatures attained enormous dimensions, and their brains grew to sizes that were equally fantastic. The brain of the bottlenose dolphin is slightly larger and just as complex in structure as that of a human being. The brains of sperm whales can be three times as large.

There is not much agreement among humans as to what goes on inside these provocatively large brains. Some authorities believe dolphins and whales possess thoughts, emotions and "languages" just as subtle and complex as those of humans, while others refuse to grant even the brightest species more intelligence than a dog or, at best, a chimpanzee. One of the most frequent arguments against cetacean intelligence is based on the idea that if they were really as smart as they appear to be, these creatures would not have

wasted so many millions of years just swimming around and enjoying themselves but would instead have created some form of material civilization. Others suggest that their not having done so is greater proof of their superior intelligence. If we ever do learn to converse with whales or dolphins, they might suggest that if we just relaxed and came back to the water we wouldn't feel the need to rush around creating so much trouble all the time.

It's a sea cow's life

The piglike ancestors of the whales and dolphins were not the only warm-blooded animals to give up the idea of life on land with intriguingly positive results. There seems to be something about ocean life that just naturally inspires high intelligence and a positive, playful, what's-your-hurry kind of attitude in mammals. Take for example the manatees and dugongs, or "sea cows" as they are sometimes called. These curious looking creatures come from completely different mammalian stock than do the dolphins and whales, but life in a marine environment has given them exceptional intelligence and a gentle, playful character that has endeared them to humans for centuries.

TIMELESS CLASSICS

The Cockroach, the Horseshoe Crab and Other Classy Creatures

On a planet like ours where so many species are here one millennium and gone the next, it's comforting to know that some creatures have successfully resisted the pressures of change for very long periods of time. The clumsy, shovel-shaped horseshoe crab, for one, has been scuttling through the seas for at least 360 million years without feeling the need to update itself. These Volkswagens of the deep are more closely related to scorpions and spiders than they are to true crabs. Their oddly successful design dates from a time when the water-dwelling ancestors of today's insects were mustering themselves for an invasion of the land. The world's first horseshoe crabs shared the seas with such outlandish and now-extinct super-bugs as the giant sea scorpion, which reached lengths of fifteen feet and hunted fish with powerful, lobsterlike claws.

The indomitable cockroach

One of the first insects to take shape, once the total conquest of land was achieved about 300 million years ago, was the cockroach. Versatile and incredibly durable, the classic cockroach is capable of weathering hardships and indignities that would wither many a lesser creature. Just about any vaguely organic substance will serve it as food, and it can live without eating anything at all for several months at a time. Recently, the cockroach's astonishing survival skills were dramatically highlighted when scientists discovered that it is virtually immune to radioactivity. If humanity decides to blow itself off the face of the earth any time in the future, the event will make little difference to the cockroach. If anything, these hard-bodied survivors would probably benefit from such a disaster, for it would leave them free to be fruitful and multiply out in the open, without fear of predatory humans and other such troublesome organisms.

Other timelessly designed, super-successful creatures on the earth today include the beetle (250 million years), the dragonfly (250 million years), the shark (350 million years) and, of course, that champion of champions, the worm (at 500 million years).

MOTHER NATURE'S
GREATEST HITS
38

SKY DIVERS

Manna from Heaven and Tumbling Toads

Throughout the centuries people have seen – or thought they've seen – a wide variety of objects and substances falling out of the skies. Most of these, like the "manna from heaven" of ancient times and the "rains of sulphur" reported more recently by fearful European peasants, may be attributed to rain storms interacting with dust clouds, wind-borne masses of pollen and similar substances. At times, however, the world's rains have delivered more substantial items.

Fish – usually small, minnowlike species but sometimes much larger ones like catfish and carp – have rained down upon surprised heads on a number of occasions throughout history. Rains of earthworms are fairly common, too, and have been reported by several individuals including one American

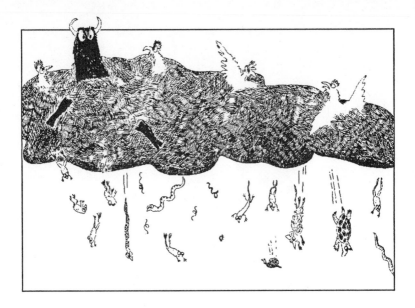

farmer who at first dismissed the event as a mirage. He changed his mind later when he removed his hat to find several of the creatures trapped in the brim.

Frogs and tadpoles, as well as toads, have also tumbled out of the sky at various times. One Roman writer of the second century A.D. describes a rain of frogs so relentless that an entire town had to be evacuated because of them. In addition to these most frequent fallers, accounts exist of rains of various types of shellfish, rats, salamanders, flightless insects of one kind or another and even an exceptionally sinister rain of snakes, some of them poisonous.

Toward the end of the nineteenth century, the city of Baton Rouge, Louisiana experienced a deluge of birds. Though it might seem less surprising to see a bird descend out of the sky than it would a frog or a rat, this event was unusual because the birds in question – ranging from sparrows to ducks to woodpeckers – did not fly down gracefully but plummeted at great speeds. All of them had apparently died long before arriving over the city. In nearby Vicksburg, Mississippi at around the same time, a gopher turtle encased in a block of ice is said to have fallen out of the skies during a hailstorm.

Natural vacuum cleaners

While in earlier times, all manner of supernatural tales were put forth to explain these phenomena, today such events are usually blamed on tornadoes and waterspouts. Tornadoes are essentially tight funnels of warm, moist air rising amid a surrounding layer of cool, descending dry air. Under the right conditions, a roving tornado can act like an oversized vacuum cleaner, sucking up everything that lies in its path from toads to church steeples and casting them back to earth several hundred yards, or many miles, away.

Tornadoes have played particularly unkind tricks on farm animals, probably because these beasts tend to be less alert to danger than their wild kin, and because they are often confined to fenced areas where escape from the path of a tornado is difficult. Cows and bulls have been picked up and spun for hundreds of yards by tornadoes. In one reliable account, a horse was levitated and torn in half.

Chickens have not only been hurled through the air at frightening speeds but actually plucked naked by intense storms. Frank W. Lane tells of an Oklahoma woman who saw the feathers from a tornado-stripped chicken driven like darts into the bark of some nearby trees. Lane also tells of buffalo being fiercely buffeted by tornadoes. He speculates that in the days when these animals roamed shoulder-to-shoulder across the prairies there may have been impressive exhibits of multiple buffalo ascensions.

MOTHER NATURE'S

GREATEST HITS

39

CREATIVE CATASTROPHES

Dinosaur Disasters and Other World-shaking Events

Horseshoe crabs and cockroaches aside, the vast majority of animal species that have come into being over the course of the earth's history are now mere memories. The earth has a tendency to play momentary favorites with its inhabitants, allowing one group of animals to flourish and diversify for a time and then sweeping most or all of them off the stage to make room for the next group. The most famous of the planet's former star-tenants are the dinosaurs, which vanished almost overnight after an extraordinarily successful stint of some 160 million years. Though no one has yet been able to prove just exactly what it was that caused the dinosaurs to disappear so suddenly and completely, most experts agree that such catastrophic exits are more or less normal here on earth. At least four major mass extinctions and many lesser ones swept the earth before the one that hit the dinosaurs – one of which killed off about ninety percent of the animal species alive on earth at the time.

Most of these planetary purges are thought to have been caused by environmental changes that took place too fast for certain species to adapt. The drift of continents, the lowering and raising of oceans, the formation and dispersal of enormous fields of glaciers – all these planetary fidgetings have had their effect on animal life. Yet some of the major extinctions occurred so suddenly that some scientists have suggested that more drastic phenomena were involved.

The great meteor shower theory

One of the most intriguing theories involves meteor showers. Some investigators say that our solar system is set up in such a way that a cloud of meteoroids, mostly circling between Mars and Jupiter, occasionally sends bursts of these celestial bodies – which can range in size from specks of dust to asteroids weighing thousands of tons – in the direction of earth. "Occasionally" means roughly every twenty-six million years, which is about the span of time estimated to have elapsed between most of the planet's mass-extinctions, as far we can determine. A major meteorite striking the surface of the earth could cause a lot of unpleasant phenomena: earthquakes, tidal waves, swirling clouds of dust that might block out the sun's life-sustaining rays for weeks or months at a time, and probably a host of other deadly complications as well.

Whatever the ultimate cause behind earth's history of devastating mass-extinctions, they seem to have been essential ingredients in the development of life as we know it. We humans, for example, would probably not be on earth today without them. By killing off almost all of the creatures in charge, these planetary shake-ups function as rough but efficient ways of allowing new ecosystems and new species to rise to positions of dominance. We mammals got our first big break in the evolutionary game ninety million years ago when the dinosaur-dominated world was suddenly left wide open for humankind to grow and diversify.

If the meteor-swarm theories are correct, the next rocky shower isn't due to arrive for about eleven million years. This means that human beings, the dominant animals of the moment, could feel quite confident about their immediate future, were it not for the fact that our species seems bent on rushing itself into extinction long before that.

BEFUDDLED BIPEDS

Anthropomorphism and Other Human Frailties

While putting together this collection, I often found myself puzzling over the problem of what to do with humans. Should I allow them into the picture of the natural world I was sketching and risk having them (as usual) push all other creatures out onto the periphery? Or should I refuse to let humans into the competition at all on the grounds that their unique and problematic intelligence sets them apart, somehow, from the rest of the natural world?

This is, of course, a very old problem, and it is basically just as open to discussion today as it was in the times of the world's first thinkers. What are we humans to make of our relationship with the rest of creation? Are we the apex of all life (as many traditional ways of thinking suggest), the culmination to which all other living organisms point, or are we instead just another animal with a coincidentally clever brain, destined like all the ingenious inventions that came before us to be swept into oblivion sooner or later? And if we are, in fact, bonafide members of the natural community and not some inexplicably alien addition to it, do we qualify as a "greatest hit," a near miss or an unmitigated flop?

In the end, I decided that it would be pretty silly to exclude humans entirely. After all, being one myself, I would inevitably end up describing animal dramas and animal behavior in terms of my own experience. Dance, play, creativity, burial of the dead...these are obviously anthropomorphic ideas. My choosing them out of an endless pool of possibilities showed that without really thinking about it, I tend to look at the natural world through a decidedly human lens. Is this necessarily a bad thing? Somehow, I don't think so. Though many scientists insist that animals must be seen in a light untainted by any human associations or human values, a totally objective point of view may be neither desirable nor possible.

Naturalists are not the only ones whose lives are intertwined with the animal kingdom. Traditional, indigenous peoples of the world often live in very close contact with wild animals and get to know their ways more intimately than most scientists could ever imagine. When we listen to such peoples talk about the ways and habits of the wild creatures they know best, we immediately notice what science would call an anthropomorphic quality to their descriptions. To an Eskimo, for example, an owl or a fox or a wolf is not an inferior organism but a fellow consciousness, capable of happiness and fear, hunger and thirst, boredom and curiosity, just as each human being is. The idea that comparisons between people and other animals are misleading and need to be avoided would strike such an individual as ridiculous. The Eskimo witnesses human kinship with the animal world on a very immediate and concrete level.

Many of the twentieth century's most perceptive students of animal behavior would agree with this traditional view of animals. According to many present-day authorities, the barrier that has long been believed to separate humans from the rest of creation is essentially an illusion. The challenge for us today is to learn to appreciate the individuality and integrity of animals without falling into the trap of simply seeing them as furry humans.

Does this mean we have to embrace Chinese liver flukes and bouncing vipers, that we have to address the cockroach and the housefly on a first-name basis? I'll leave such knotty considerations to the reader...

BIBLIOGRAPHY

Choosing material for a catalog of the natural world's wonders is a potentially overwhelming prospect, even when one has admitted to oneself ahead of time that there won't be a chance of collecting more than a random handful. Wandering in a daze through the Nature and Science sections of various libraries, I often felt like one of those game-show contestants set loose in a department store with only sixty seconds to grab all the merchandise he or she wants. Though each of the books listed below was helpful in one way or another, I owe a special debt to a few volumes in particular. These books not only supplied me with a larger than average number of usable tidbits, but also provided me with a number of general insights that made the task of organizing my material much easier.

Sally Carrighar's *Wild Heritage* and Jacques Graven's *Non-Human Thought* – both written in the 1960s – are still two of the best popular overviews of animal behavior available, and anyone who finds the material contained in this book interesting would probably enjoy them as well. Maurice Burton's *Just Like an Animal*, an investigation of the potentials of animal intelligence, also contains an extraordinary amount of interesting material. As far as general compendiums of oddities in the natural world, William Corliss has assembled several, each of which are brimming with bizarre and enlightening excerpts taken from a wide variety of sources. For animals that either are or are supposed to be "dangerous to man," Roger Caras' book of the same name is probably the best general reference, while for straightforward animal superlatives (fastest, slowest, smartest, heaviest, etc.) nothing beats Gerald L. Wood's *Animal Facts and Feats*, published as part of the Guinness series.

BOOKS

Andrews, Roy Chapman. *This Amazing Planet*. Putnam, 1940.

Amory, Cleveland. *Animail*. Windmill Books, 1976.

Bates, Marston. *The Forest and the Sea: A Look at the Economy of Nature and the Ecology of Man*. Random House, 1960.

Borror, Donald J. and White, Richard E. *A Field Guide to the Insects of North America and Mexico*. Peterson Field Guide Series, Houghton Mifflin, 1970.

Breland, Osmond P. *Animal Life and Lore*. Harper & Row, 1972.

Brown, Vinson. *Sea Mammals and Reptiles of the Pacific Coast*. Collier Books, 1976.

Burton, Maurice. *Just Like an Animal*. Scribner's, 1978.

Cahalane, Victor. *Mammals of North America*. Macmillan, 1961.

Caras, Roger. *The Custer Wolf: Biography of an American Renegade*. Holt, Rinehart and Winston, 1979.

_____. *Dangerous to Man: The Definitive Story of Wildlife's Reputed Dangers*. Revised edition, Holt, Rinehart and Winston, 1976.

_____. *The Private Lives of Animals*. Grosset and Dunlap, 1976.

Carrighar, Sally. *Wild Heritage*. Houghton Mifflin, 1965.

Collins, W.B. *Empires in Anarchy*. MacGibbon & Kee, 1967. (A general treatment of ants and termites.)

Corliss, William. *Strange Phenomena*. (Most of my material on animal rains came from an article reprinted here by Waldo L. McAtee, "Showers of Organic Matter.") The Sourcebook Project, 1974.

_____. *Incredible Life: A Handbook of Biological Mysteries*. Sourcebook Project, 1981. (Much of my singing mouse material, including the quoted passages, came from materials included here.)

Cruickshank, Allan and Helen. *1001 Questions Answered About Birds*. Dover, 1976.

Davids, Richard C. *Lords of the Arctic*. Collier Macmillan, 1982. (An excellent, very readable polar bear source.)

Devoe, Alan. *This Fascinating Animal World*. McGraw Hill, 1951. (A dated but quite comprehensive collection of material presented in question-and-answer format.)

Dinsdale, Tim. *The Leviathans*. Routledge & Keegan Paul, 1966. (Ogopongo, Manipogo and associates.)

_____. *The Loch Ness Monster*. Routledge & Keegan Paul, 1961.

Dufresne, Frank. *No Room for Bears*. Holt, Rinehart and Winston, 1965.

Eldridge, Niles. *Life Pulse*. Facts on File, 1987.

Emiliani, Cesare. *The Scientific Companion: Exploring the Physical World With Facts, Figures and Formulas*. Wiley Science Editions, 1988.

Forsyth, Adrian and Miyata, Ken. *Tropical Nature*. Scribner's, 1984. (A well written overview of the ecology of tropical jungles and rain forests – specifically those in Central and South America.)

George, Jean Craighead. *Beastly Inventions: A Surprising Investigation into How Smart Animals Really Are*. D. McKay, 1970. (A rich source of odds and ends.)

Graven, Jacques. *Non-Human Thought: The Mysteries of the Animal Psyche*. Translated from the French by Harold J. Salemson. Stein & Day, Inc., 1967.

Grzimek, Dr. H. C. Bernhard (gen. ed.) *Grzimek's Animal Life Encyclopedia*.

Hall, Angus. *Monsters and Mythical Beasts*. Doubleday, 1976.

Hendrickson, Robert. *The Ocean Almanac*. Doubleday, 1984. (An enormous collection of odds and ends relating to various aspects of the world's oceans.)

Herald, Earl S. *Fishes of North America*. Doubleday, 1972.

_____. *Living Fishes of the World*. Doubleday, 1961.

Jenkins, Allan C. *Mysteries of Nature*. Facts on File, 1984.

Krutch, Joseph Wood. *The Desert Year*. University of Arizona Press, 1985.

_____. *The Great Chain of Life*. Houghton Mifflin, 1977.

Lane, Frank W. *Animal Wonder World: A Chronicle of the Unusual in Nature*. Sheridan House, 1951. (Lots of weird stuff to be found here.)

_____. *The Kingdom of the Octopus: The Life History of the Cephalopoda*. Sheridan House, 1960.

_____. *The Violent Earth*. Salem House, 1986.

Lineweaver, Thomas and Backus, Richard. *The Natural History of Sharks*. Lyons & Burford, 1986. (Definitely the best popular book on sharks available.)

Lopez, Barry Holstun. *Of Wolves and Men*. Scribner's, 1978. (A popular investigation of the natural history of wolves and their interactions with humans over the centuries.)

Lorenz, Konrad Z. *King Solomon's Ring: New Light on Animal Ways.* Harper Torchbooks, 1976. (The insights and discoveries of the century's greatest student of animal behavior presented in an informal style.)

McFarland, David. *The Oxford Companion to Animal Behavior.* Oxford University Press, 1987.

McIntyre, Joan. *Mind in the Waters: A Book to Celebrate the Consciousness of Whales and Dolphins.* Scribner's, 1974.

McNally, Robert. *So Remorseless a Havoc.* Little, Brown, 1981. (One of the best popular accounts of the life of whales and dolphins and how humans perceive them.)

Minton, Sherman A. and Minton, Madge Rutherford. *Giant Reptiles.* Scribner's, 1973.

Morris, Desmond. *Animalwatching.* Crown Publishers, 1990.

Murchie, Guy. *The Seven Mysteries of Life.* Houghton Mifflin, 1978. (An unpretentious and far-ranging exploration of life on earth. Lengthy, but worth the time.)

Ogburn, Charlton. *The Adventure of Birds.* Morrow, 1976. (A good, informal exploration of the world of birds.)

Orr, Robert T. *The Animal Kingdom.* MacMillan, 1965.

_____. *Mammals of North America.* Doubleday, 1971.

Pryor, Karen. *Lands Before the Wind: Adventures in Porpoise Training.* Harper & Row, 1975.

Quammen, David. *Natural Acts: A Sidelong View of Science and Nature.* Schocken, 1985.

Ricciutti, Edward R. *Killers of the Seas.* Walker, 1973.

Rood, Ronald. *Animals Nobody Loves.* Steven Greene Press, 1971.

Scheffer, Victor. *The Year of the Whale.* Scribner's, 1969. (This much-read book mixes facts about whales and whaling with a fictionalized account of a year in the life of a young sperm whale. See also Scheffer's companion volume, *The Year of the Seal.*)

The editors of *Scientific American. Twentieth Century Bestiary.* Simon & Schuster, 1955. (A collection of essays, many of them still worthwhile, on the general topic of animal behavior. Much of my shrew material was taken from an essay by Oliver Pearson included here.)

Sheldrake, Rupert. *The Presence of the Past.* Vintage, 1989. (A controversial re-examination of the shortcomings of evolutionary theory in the light of new insights into the way nature works and "thinks.")

Simon, Hilda. *The Courtship of Birds.* Dodd, Mead, 1977.

Small, George S. *The Blue Whale.* Columbia University Press, 1971.

Sweeney, James B. *Pictorial History of Sea Monsters and Other Dangerous Marine Life.* Crown, 1972.

Ternes, Alan (ed.). *Ants, Indians and Little Dinosaurs.* Scribner's, 1975. (A collection of essays from *Natural History* magazine. Includes good material on coyotes, mosquitoes, killer whales, and ice age mammals, especially mammoths.)

Tinbergen, Niko and the editors of Time-Life Books. *Animal Behavior.* Time Life Books, 1965.

Walker, Braz. *Oddball Fishes and Other Strange Creatures of the Deep.* Sterling Publishing Co., 1975.

Went, Herbert. *The Sex Life of the Animals.* Translated from the German by Richard and Clara Winston. Simon and Schuster, 1965.

Weyer, Edward, Jr. *The Strangest Creatures on Earth.* Sheridan House, 1953.

Wilford, John Noble. *The Riddle of the Dinosaur.* Vintage, 1986. (An up-to-date examination of dinosaur facts and falsehoods and the revolutions in the world of dinosaur study that have been occurring over the past few years.)

Wood, Gerald L. *Animal Facts and Feats,* revised 2nd edition. Sterling Publishing Co., 1977.

ARTICLES

Boraiko, Allen A. "The Indomitable Cockroach" in *National Geographic.* January, 1981.

Chaffer, Norman. "Australia's Amazing Bowerbirds" in *National Geographic.* December, 1961.

Gore, Rick. "Extinctions" in *National Geographic.* June, 1989.

Haskins, Caryl P. "The Ant and Her World" in *National Geographic.* June, 1984.

Hollander, Bert. "The Wonderfully Diverse Ways of the Ant" in *National Geographic.* June, 1984.

May, Alan G. "The Elusive Sea Otter" reprinted from *Natural History* in *The Strangest Creatures on Earth.*

Rudlow, Anne and Jack. "The Changeless Horseshoe Crab" in *National Geographic.* April 1981.

Look for these other titles from Living Planet Press

The Rainforest Book:
How you can save the world's rainforests
by Scott Lewis with a preface by Robert Redford
> Every person's window into the spectacular world of tropical rainforests – their amazing diversity, the threats to their survival, and the ways we can preserve them for future generations. $5.95

Saving Our Ancient Forests
by Seth Zuckerman
> This concise, information-packed handbook transports you to the majestic old-growth forests of the Pacific Northwest where giant redwoods and Douglas firs tower above one of nature's oldest and most complex ecosystems. $5.95

The Animal Rights Handbook:
Everyday ways to save animal lives
> The first step-by-step guide to saving animal lives in simple, everyday ways. Find out how and where to buy humane products, tips on protecting endangered wildlife and preventing animal cruelty, and easy ways to speak out for animal justice. $4.95

And for kids who will have fun learning while they color:

Color the Rainforest $4.95

Color the Ancient Forest $4.95

Sharing the Planet with Animals:
An endangered wildlife coloring book $4.95

Available in your local bookstore. For information about discounts on bulk orders, call Living Planet Press at (213) 396-0188.

Three Decades of Local Victories and Global Leadership

For 30 years, World Wildlife Fund has been working to protect the earth's endangered wildlife and wildlands and to safeguard the natural resources upon which all life depends. WWF is the largest international conservation organization in the world, with 28 affiliates on five continents and a membership of more than 1,000,000 in the United States alone.

WWF has sponsored more than 3,000 conservation projects in 140 wildlife-rich countries, leading the international drive to:

- defend embattled tropical forests from deforestation
- rescue endangered species from extinction
- establish and protect national parks and reserves
- help meet the needs of local peoples without destroying their surroundings
- curb illegal trade in rare species
- train and equip rangers, guards and anti-poaching teams
- sponsor scientific investigations that spark protective actions

World Wildlife Fund is dedicated to winning the life-and-death race to protect the world's wildlife and the rich biological diversity that they – and we – need to survive.

Although we cannot single-handedly win the battle, we can lead the way. From fighting to save a single species in a remote rain forest to marshalling support for international conservation agreements, WWF members, affiliates and allies are changing the world.

If you'd like to join in our efforts, please write for information to:

In the United States

World Wildlife Fund
Department ZF23
1250 Twenty-fourth Street, NW
Washington, DC 20037

WWF

In Canada

World Wildlife Fund Canada
90 Eglinton Avenue East
Suite 504
Toronto, Ontario M4 P2Z7

World Wildlife Fund
Membership Contribution Form

YES, I want to join World Wildlife Fund and support its efforts to save the world's endangered species and their habitats whenever and wherever they are threatened.

I've enclosed a tax-deductible contribution of:

☐ $15 Member ☐ $25 Friend ☐ $50 Associate

☐ $100 Contributor ☐ $250 Sponsor ☐ $500 Sustainer

☐ $1,000 Partner in Conservation

☐ I am already a member, but I am enclosing a tax-deductible contribution of $_____ .

Name _____

☐ Mr. ☐ Mrs. ☐ Ms. ☐ Mr. and Mrs.

Address _____

City _____ State _____ Zip _____

Note: A gift of $15 or more entitles you to 12 months of membership with all benefits listed below. Please enclose your tax-deductible check, made to WORLD WILDLIFE FUND, along with this form and return to:

World Wildlife Fund
Department ZF23
1250 Twenty-fourth Street, NW
Washington, DC 20037
WWF

WORLD WILDLIFE FUND Member Benefits:

- Six issues of FOCUS, WWF's members-only newsletter filled with photographs and articles on the latest wildlife action projects.
- Official personalized membership card with distinctive WWF logo.
- Opportunities to visit WWF conservation sites and to learn about projects first-hand in the company of WWF staff.
- Invitations to lectures in your area by WWF scientists and field staff.
- The satisfaction of knowing that you are doing your part to help protect the natural diversity of life on Earth.